Faith Moves Kingdom Come Planner
(Kingdom Come Book Series)
Published by Kingdom Come Group LLC
1701 Upland Drive, Houston TX 77043

Unless otherwise noted, Scripture quotations are taken from the Holy Bible
"King James Version." © 1982 by Thomas Nelson. All rights reserved.

ISBN: 978-1-7362728-0-0
First edition: December 2020

Most Kingdom Come books are available at special discounts for bulk
purchase, sale promotions, premiums, fund-raising, or educational use at
kingdomcomemusic.org

A man's heart plans his way,
but the Lord directs his steps

This planner belongs to

_____

If found please Email or call

_____

Note from Author

God has great plans in store for you. There's only one you! God created you specifically for such a time as this and He has a great purpose for your life! His thoughts and plans for you are good, to prosper you and bring you to an expected destination. Remember, God is for you, not against you! Distractions from the enemy can cause us to be deceived, faithless, wavering in unbelief and unfruitful. We must intentionally decide to cooperate with our God given faith and God's word; truth. Remember, as children of God we are partakers of God's divine nature and we have the authority. As we believe God we begin to walk in the revelation of our true identity as the redeemed new creation through Christ's finished work. With this foundation we can approach every problem, decision, plan, goal, and dream from the stance of total victory!

I created this productivity planner to help inspire, mobilize, encourage, nurture and manifest God's very best in life. On your journey let this be a tool to help you write the vision down and execute the dreams God has placed in your heart. Expect and plan for advancement, and fruitfulness. Be ready to walk in everything that belongs to you as God's precious child knowing that He is able, willing, and He has already finished the work.

As you cooperate with your God given faith, and the truth; God's Holy word, His holy spirt will lead and empower you to fulfill His will, execute every assignment with grace and advance His kingdom in the earth as it is in heaven!

Amber Camp

Core Values

The first step is to adopt a biblical world view as your foundation. Our dreams executed should express the heart of God. This means our goals that support our big dreams will be shaped by core values that align with our identity in Christ. As we realize our true identity as children of God, we can focus on values that yield fruitfulness!

Circle values you already thrive in
Underline values you want to work toward

authenticity

gratitude

Spiritual Growth

respect

wealth

community

integrity

patience   loyalty

courage

compassion

authority

purity

generosity

confidence

productivity

excellence   maturity

perseverance

discipline

professionalism

accountability   **soberness**

self control

Self-Reflections

It is important to know God, know yourself and know others that labor among you! Realizing truths about yourself and others can help you prioritize, focus and create healthy boundaries. This further promotes creativity, and productivity.

As you reflect on these questions, by faith look forward to where God is taking you and acknowledge where there is room for change and growth.

Who am I today? What roles do I play?

Who do I want to be?

God's call and purpose for my life is:

Personal wins or accomplishments of mine so far:

I feel accomplished or fulfilled when:

I enjoy myself when:

I am my authentic self when:

I am in strife when:

I worry when:

I'm at peace when:

Prophesies Spoken over me:

Define the "good life". What does joy and contentment look like for you?

Dreams/Visions List

Write the vision and make it plain
so that people can run with it!

God has created you for purpose and placed dreams in your heart. Then declare those things that are not as though they are! Be confident that through Jesus, you have all of the time, money, resources, ability, favor, and people to do in excellence what God has called you to do! DREAM BIG!

Big Dream/ Vision Discription	Scriptural backing and purpose: why is this important to me? How does this dream fulfill God's call on my life?	Date/Testimony of Manifestation

Big Dream/ Vision Discription	Scriptural backing and purpose: why is this important to me? How does this dream fulfill God's call on my life?	Date/Testimony of Manifestation

Life Trajectory

DREAM AGAIN! Take a look back at your Dreams list. Remember not to get overwhelmed. God's timing is the best timing, and If your dreams don't scare you, they aren't big enough! Think about a timeline for your dreams and ask the Holy Spirit to help you as you begin to plan.
Where do you see yourself today, in 1 year, 5 years, 10 years, 100 year-legacy? Only what you do for Christ will last.

	1 Year	5 Year	10 Year	100 Years Legacy
What do I do for work?				
Where do I stand financially?				
How do I spend most of my time?				
What are important aspirations visions and goals?				
How do I impact and bless the community and world?				
Relationships I prioritize and value				

$\mathcal{D}$eclaration over my life & $\mathcal{P}$rayer

Life and death are in the power of the tongue. God's word does not profit us unless it's mixed with faith! Let's take our God given faith and cooperate with the truth; God's word!

Say this out loud;
I can do all things through Christ who strengthens Me!
I am empowered by the indwelling of the Holy Spirit!
I am the righteousness of God through Jesus
I am the head and not the tail
I am above, not beneath
I am the lender, not the borrower
I am ahead, not behind
I am an ambush
and I am an answer to prayer
I am His called

$\mathcal{P}$rayer

Father,
Thank you for loving me perfectly and forgiving me completely. Today I choose to focus on you above all things. I renounce the enemy and I choose to cooperate with your word and Jesus's finished work for me. I believe and prioritize your report over any other information. You've created me for purposed and you will fulfill my days.
I walk by faith, not by sight. I will not look back and get discouraged, distracted or defeated by loss. I am not overwhelmed, I am empowered by you. You will restore the years the locust stole, make up for missed opportunities, and even lost time! You are the Lord my healer. Thank you for working what the enemy meant to destroy me all for my good, all the time! You will perfect those things concerning me! Thank you for fresh revelation of your word each day! I love you.
Amen

Acknowledge the Lord in all your ways and He will direct your path.

Example page: How to use this planner

Your days will be organized to accomplish Goal tasks, and your daily routine tasks. To establish your goals you will take a look back at your Dreams & Vision list and your life trajectory page. With guidance from the Holy Spirit, prioritize what feels more urgent to start working towards first! Come up with monthly goals that support the Big dreams & Vision. Then break down those goals into smaller tasks to complete daily.
  Below is an example.

Dream   Be an Impactful
           Author

Goal	Tasks
Finish writing my 1st Book!	Finish writing chapter 3
	Purchase publishing scan code
	Find illustration for book cover

One of your big dreams could be "to be an impactful author." A goal that supports this dream would be to actually "finish writing a book!" This goal can be broken down into smaller achievable "tasks" like; "finish writing a chapter", "purchase scan codes for publishing" or "find and hire an illustrator to design the book cover". You can prioritize and complete these tasks that will help you achieve the goals that support Big Dreams/vision.

Weekly Goal Tasks & Daily Routine Tasks Example page

Look back at your month Goals and choose tasks for this week to execute. As you complete the tasks you will check them off on your daily outlook pages. At the end of the week and month you can check off if you have completed the goals and tasks.

Week: 14/09/20 to 20/09/20

Goal Tasks   Routine tasks

Goal Tasks	Routine tasks
Purchase scan code for publishing	Prayer/Devotion time with God
Meet with illustrator for book cover	Work out
Write Chapter 3	Fold Laundry
Create website for book	Meal prep/ Cook dinner

After establishing your weekly tasks, choose what goal tasks you will work on today, track routine task completion and give yourself a productivity score.

Monday   14/09/20

Schedual Notes

Meet with illustrator 3pm

Writing block 5-6pm

Rehearsal 7pm

Goal Tasks

Find illustrator for book cover

Write chapter 3

Productivity Score

✓ **Routine Tasks completed** (1)(2)(3)(4)(5) 6 (7)(8)(9)(10)

Let's Get Started!

And let us not be weary in well doing:
for in due season we shall reap, if we faint not.
It's time to get started! Here are some things
we can abandon on our productive path!

-Abandon distractions

Your goal tasks or routine tasks for the day will require you to be intentional about creating space and uninterrupted time to execute, complete and move forward. This may mean turning off notifications or shutting down social media apps on your phone during allotted times. You may need to brief family and friends to call you before or after that time. You may need to set up a specific schedule for those who depend on you, so you know exactly how they will be occupied during that time slot. Remember, you can do all things through Christ who strengthens you. God is in you, so you already have everything you need.

-Abandon doubt

Nothing limits you more than your own thinking. As a man thinks in his heart, so is he. Your dreams are possible, remember with God all things are possible. Whatever you want to see happen in your life, see it, visualize it and don't be double minded; only believe. Don't wait for others to believe in your dream. Go forward on what God speaks and thinks of you!
Let your confidence, assurance and validation come from Him and no one else.

-Abandon comparison

Comparison is often the number one thing keeping you from doing what God has called you to do it causes us to be deceived out of God's best for us. A funny but true quote comes to mind; "Be yourself, everyone else is taken!". Turn your coveting and intimidation into gratitude and inspiration. You can use other's experiences for encouragement, but don't compare your identity, calling or path with others. Your differences will be the very thing God uses in unique ways to touch people's lives. Remember, God knew you before He formed you in your mother's womb. You are fearfully and wonderfully made!

-Abandon excuses

We can always find reasons not to pursue dreams and goals that God has placed in our heart. Excuses are subtle reasons we cooperate with to justify why we can't succeed. Excuses allow us to settle for less than God's best.

Prayer:

Lord, As I prepare to be intentional with the time that you've given me, help me to prioritize and complete all you have called me to do, from daily routine tasks to the visions and dreams you have placed in my heart.

Month: _____

Sunday	Monday	Tuesday	Wednesday	Thursday	Friday	Saturday

Monthly Goals

Dream

Goal

Tasks

_____

Dream

Goal

Tasks

_____

Dream

Goal

Tasks

Monthly Goals

Goal

Tasks

_____
_____

_____
_____
_____
_____
_____
_____

Goal

Tasks

_____
_____

_____
_____
_____
_____
_____
_____

Goal

Tasks

_____
_____
_____
_____
_____
_____

JOHN 15:5
"I AM THE VINE; YOU ARE THE BRANCHES. IF YOU REMAIN IN ME AND I IN YOU, YOU WILL BEAR MUCH FRUIT; APART FROM ME YOU CAN DO NOTHING.

$\mathcal{W}$eek: _____

Goal Tasks	Routine Tasks
(order of priority)	

Goal Tasks:
_____
_____
_____
_____
_____
_____
_____
_____
_____
_____
_____
_____
_____

Monday _____

Schedual Notes

Goal Tasks
_____
_____
_____
_____

Productivity Score

Routine Tasks completed (1)(2)(3)(4)(5)(6)(7)(8)(9)(10)

Tuesday _____

Schedual Notes

Goal Tasks
_____
_____
_____
_____

Productivity Score

Routine Tasks completed (1)(2)(3)(4)(5)(6)(7)(8)(9)(10)

Wednesday_____

Schedual Notes

Goal Tasks
_____
_____
_____
_____

Productivity Score

Routine Tasks completed (1)(2)(3)(4)(5)(6)(7)(8)(9)(10)

Thursday _____

Schedual Notes

Goal Tasks
_____
_____
_____
_____

Productivity Score

Routine Tasks completed (1)(2)(3)(4)(5)(6)(7)(8)(9)(10)

Friday _____

Schedual Notes

Goal Tasks

_____
_____
_____
_____

Productivity Score

Routine Tasks completed ①②③④⑤⑥⑦⑧⑨⑩

Saturday _____

Schedual Notes

Goal Tasks

_____
_____
_____
_____

Productivity Score

Routine Tasks completed ①②③④⑤⑥⑦⑧⑨⑩

Sunday _____

Schedual Notes

Goal Tasks

_____
_____
_____
_____

Productivity Score

Routine Tasks completed ①②③④⑤⑥⑦⑧⑨⑩

Weekly Reflection

Weekly wins; What went well?

What routine tasks or goal tasks were not completed and why?

What have you learned? What would you change?

PROVERBS 29:18
WHERE THERE IS NO VISION,
THE PEOPLE PERISH...

Week: _____

Goal Tasks (order of priority)	Routine Tasks
_____	
_____	
_____	
_____	
_____	
_____	
_____	
_____	
_____	
_____	
_____	
_____	
_____	

Monday _____ **Goal Tasks**

Schedual Notes

_____

_____

_____

_____

Productivity Score

Routine Tasks completed ①②③④⑤⑥⑦⑧⑨⑩

Tuesday _____ **Goal Tasks**

Schedual Notes

_____

_____

_____

_____

Productivity Score

Routine Tasks completed ①②③④⑤⑥⑦⑧⑨⑩

Wednesday _____ **Goal Tasks**

Schedual Notes

_____

_____

_____

_____

Productivity Score

Routine Tasks completed ①②③④⑤⑥⑦⑧⑨⑩

Thursday _____ **Goal Tasks**

Schedual Notes

_____

_____

_____

_____

Productivity Score

Routine Tasks completed ①②③④⑤⑥⑦⑧⑨⑩

Friday _____ **Goal Tasks**

    Schedual Notes
_____
_____
_____
_____

Productivity Score

Routine Tasks completed ①②③④⑤⑥⑦⑧⑨⑩

Saturday _____ **Goal Tasks**

    Schedual Notes
_____
_____
_____
_____

Productivity Score

Routine Tasks completed ①②③④⑤⑥⑦⑧⑨⑩

Sunday _____ **Goal Tasks**

    Schedual Notes
_____
_____
_____
_____

Productivity Score

Routine Tasks completed ①②③④⑤⑥⑦⑧⑨⑩

Weekly Reflection

Weekly wins; What went well?

What routine tasks or goal tasks were not completed and why?

What have you learned? What would you change?

ROMANS 8:28
AND WE KNOW THAT ALL THINGS WORK TOGETHER FOR GOOD TO THEM THAT LOVE GOD, TO THEM WHO ARE THE CALLED ACCORDING TO HIS PURPOSE.

Week: _____

Goal Tasks
(order of priority)

Routine Tasks

_____

_____

_____

_____

_____

_____

_____

_____

_____

_____

_____

_____

_____

_____

Monday ——————————— **Goal Tasks**

    Schedual Notes

    ————————————

    ————————————

    ————————————

Productivity Score

Routine Tasks completed ① ② ③ ④ ⑤ ⑥ ⑦ ⑧ ⑨ ⑩

Tuesday ——————————— **Goal Tasks**

    Schedual Notes

    ————————————

    ————————————

    ————————————

Productivity Score

Routine Tasks completed ① ② ③ ④ ⑤ ⑥ ⑦ ⑧ ⑨ ⑩

Wednesday——————————— **Goal Tasks**

    Schedual Notes

    ————————————

    ————————————

    ————————————

Productivity Score

Routine Tasks completed ① ② ③ ④ ⑤ ⑥ ⑦ ⑧ ⑨ ⑩

Thursday ——————————— **Goal Tasks**

    Schedual Notes

    ————————————

    ————————————

    ————————————

Productivity Score

Routine Tasks completed ① ② ③ ④ ⑤ ⑥ ⑦ ⑧ ⑨ ⑩

Friday _____

Schedual Notes

Goal Tasks

_____
_____
_____
_____

Productivity Score

Routine Tasks completed (1)(2)(3)(4)(5)(6)(7)(8)(9)(10)

Saturday _____

Schedual Notes

Goal Tasks

_____
_____
_____
_____

Productivity Score

Routine Tasks completed (1)(2)(3)(4)(5)(6)(7)(8)(9)(10)

Sunday _____

Schedual Notes

Goal Tasks

_____
_____
_____
_____

Productivity Score

Routine Tasks completed (1)(2)(3)(4)(5)(6)(7)(8)(9)(10)

Weekly Reflection

Weekly wins; What went well?

What routine tasks or goal tasks were not completed and why?

What have you learned? What would you change?

PSALM 37:5
COMMIT THY WAY UNTO THE LORD; TRUST ALSO IN HIM; AND HE SHALL BRING IT TO PASS.

Week: _____

Goal Tasks
(order of priority)

_____
_____
_____
_____
_____
_____
_____
_____
_____
_____
_____
_____

Routine Tasks

Monday _____   **Goal Tasks**

    Schedual Notes _____

_____

_____

_____

Productivity Score

Routine Tasks completed ① ② ③ ④ ⑤ ⑥ ⑦ ⑧ ⑨ ⑩

Tuesday _____   **Goal Tasks**

    Schedual Notes _____

_____

_____

_____

Productivity Score

Routine Tasks completed ① ② ③ ④ ⑤ ⑥ ⑦ ⑧ ⑨ ⑩

Wednesday _____   **Goal Tasks**

    Schedual Notes _____

_____

_____

_____

Productivity Score

Routine Tasks completed ① ② ③ ④ ⑤ ⑥ ⑦ ⑧ ⑨ ⑩

Thursday _____   **Goal Tasks**

    Schedual Notes _____

_____

_____

_____

Productivity Score

Routine Tasks completed ① ② ③ ④ ⑤ ⑥ ⑦ ⑧ ⑨ ⑩

Friday _____   **Goal Tasks**

     Schedual Notes

_____

_____

_____

_____

Productivity Score

Routine Tasks completed ①②③④⑤⑥⑦⑧⑨⑩

Saturday _____   **Goal Tasks**

     Schedual Notes

_____

_____

_____

_____

Productivity Score

Routine Tasks completed ①②③④⑤⑥⑦⑧⑨⑩

Sunday _____   **Goal Tasks**

     Schedual Notes

_____

_____

_____

_____

Productivity Score

Routine Tasks completed ①②③④⑤⑥⑦⑧⑨⑩

Weekly Reflection

Weekly wins; What went well?

What routine tasks or goal tasks were not completed and why?

What have you learned? What would you change?

Month: _____

Sunday	Monday	Tuesday	Wednesday	Thursday	Friday	Saturday

Monthly Goals

Goal

Tasks

Goal

Tasks

Goal

Tasks

Monthly Goals

Dream

Goal   Tasks

Dream

Goal   Tasks

Dream

Goal   Tasks

ROMANS 8:31
WHAT SHALL WE THEN SAY TO THESE THINGS? IF GOD BE FOR US, WHO CAN BE AGAINST US?

Week: _____

Goal Tasks (order of priority)	Routine Tasks
_____	
_____	
_____	
_____	
_____	
_____	
_____	
_____	
_____	
_____	
_____	
_____	
_____	
_____	

Monday _____

Schedual Notes

Goal Tasks

_____
_____
_____
_____

Productivity Score

Routine Tasks completed ①②③④⑤⑥⑦⑧⑨⑩

Tuesday _____

Schedual Notes

Goal Tasks

_____
_____
_____
_____

Productivity Score

Routine Tasks completed ①②③④⑤⑥⑦⑧⑨⑩

Wednesday _____

Schedual Notes

Goal Tasks

_____
_____
_____
_____

Productivity Score

Routine Tasks completed ①②③④⑤⑥⑦⑧⑨⑩

Thursday _____

Schedual Notes

Goal Tasks

_____
_____
_____
_____

Productivity Score

Routine Tasks completed ①②③④⑤⑥⑦⑧⑨⑩

Friday _____ **Goal Tasks**

    Schedual Notes
_____

_____

_____

_____

Productivity Score

Routine Tasks completed ①②③④⑤⑥⑦⑧⑨⑩

Saturday _____ **Goal Tasks**

    Schedual Notes
_____

_____

_____

_____

Productivity Score

Routine Tasks completed ①②③④⑤⑥⑦⑧⑨⑩

Sunday _____ **Goal Tasks**

    Schedual Notes
_____

_____

_____

_____

Productivity Score

Routine Tasks completed ①②③④⑤⑥⑦⑧⑨⑩

Weekly Reflection

Weekly wins; What went well?

What routine tasks or goal tasks were not completed and why?

What have you learned? What would you change?

PSALM 121:2
MY HELP COMETH FROM THE LORD, WHICH MADE HEAVEN AND EARTH.

$\mathcal{W}$eek: _____

Goal Tasks
(order of priority)

Routine Tasks

_____
_____
_____
_____
_____
_____
_____
_____
_____
_____
_____
_____
_____
_____
_____

Monday _____ **Goal Tasks**

Schedual Notes _____

_____

_____

_____

Productivity Score

Routine Tasks completed ①②③④⑤⑥⑦⑧⑨⑩

Tuesday _____ **Goal Tasks**

Schedual Notes _____

_____

_____

_____

Productivity Score

Routine Tasks completed ①②③④⑤⑥⑦⑧⑨⑩

Wednesday_____ **Goal Tasks**

Schedual Notes _____

_____

_____

_____

Productivity Score

Routine Tasks completed ①②③④⑤⑥⑦⑧⑨⑩

Thursday _____ **Goal Tasks**

Schedual Notes _____

_____

_____

_____

Productivity Score

Routine Tasks completed ①②③④⑤⑥⑦⑧⑨⑩

Friday _____

Schedual Notes

Goal Tasks

_____
_____
_____
_____

Productivity Score

Routine Tasks completed ①②③④⑤⑥⑦⑧⑨⑩

Saturday _____

Schedual Notes

Goal Tasks

_____
_____
_____
_____

Productivity Score

Routine Tasks completed ①②③④⑤⑥⑦⑧⑨⑩

Sunday _____

Schedual Notes

Goal Tasks

_____
_____
_____
_____

Productivity Score

Routine Tasks completed ①②③④⑤⑥⑦⑧⑨⑩

Weekly Reflection

Weekly wins; What went well?

What routine tasks or goal tasks were not completed and why?

What have you learned? What would you change?

PHILIPPIANS 4:13
I CAN DO ALL THINGS THROUGH CHRIST WHICH STRENGTHENETH ME.

Week: _____

Goal Tasks
(order of priority)

_____
_____
_____
_____
_____
_____
_____
_____
_____
_____
_____
_____
_____
_____

Routine Tasks

Monday _____ **Goal Tasks**

Schedual Notes

_____

_____

_____

_____

Productivity Score

Routine Tasks completed ①②③④⑤⑥⑦⑧⑨⑩

Tuesday _____ **Goal Tasks**

Schedual Notes

_____

_____

_____

_____

Productivity Score

Routine Tasks completed ①②③④⑤⑥⑦⑧⑨⑩

Wednesday _____ **Goal Tasks**

Schedual Notes

_____

_____

_____

_____

Productivity Score

Routine Tasks completed ①②③④⑤⑥⑦⑧⑨⑩

Thursday _____ **Goal Tasks**

Schedual Notes

_____

_____

_____

_____

Productivity Score

Routine Tasks completed ①②③④⑤⑥⑦⑧⑨⑩

Friday _____

Schedual Notes

Goal Tasks

_____
_____
_____
_____

Productivity Score

Routine Tasks completed ①②③④⑤⑥⑦⑧⑨⑩

Saturday _____

Schedual Notes

Goal Tasks

_____
_____
_____
_____

Productivity Score

Routine Tasks completed ①②③④⑤⑥⑦⑧⑨⑩

Sunday _____

Schedual Notes

Goal Tasks

_____
_____
_____
_____

Productivity Score

Routine Tasks completed ①②③④⑤⑥⑦⑧⑨⑩

Weekly Reflection

Weekly wins; What went well?

What routine tasks or goal tasks were not completed and why?

What have you learned? What would you change?

MARK 9:23
JESUS SAID UNTO HIM, IF THOU CANST BELIEVE, ALL THINGS ARE POSSIBLE TO HIM THAT BELIE-VETH.

Week: _____

Goal Tasks
(order of priority)

Routine Tasks

_____

_____

_____

_____

_____

_____

_____

_____

_____

_____

_____

_____

_____

Monday _____   **Goal Tasks**

   Schedual Notes   _____

                                          _____

                                          _____

                                          _____

                                          Productivity Score

Routine Tasks completed ① ② ③ ④ ⑤ ⑥ ⑦ ⑧ ⑨ ⑩

Tuesday _____   **Goal Tasks**

   Schedual Notes   _____

                                          _____

                                          _____

                                          _____

                                          _____

                                          Productivity Score

Routine Tasks completed ① ② ③ ④ ⑤ ⑥ ⑦ ⑧ ⑨ ⑩

Wednesday_____   **Goal Tasks**

   Schedual Notes   _____

                                          _____

                                          _____

                                          _____

                                          _____

                                          Productivity Score

Routine Tasks completed ① ② ③ ④ ⑤ ⑥ ⑦ ⑧ ⑨ ⑩

Thursday _____   **Goal Tasks**

   Schedual Notes   _____

                                          _____

                                          _____

                                          _____

                                          _____

                                          Productivity Score

Routine Tasks completed ① ② ③ ④ ⑤ ⑥ ⑦ ⑧ ⑨ ⑩

Friday _____   **Goal Tasks**

    Schedual Notes
_____

_____

_____

_____

                          Productivity Score

Routine Tasks completed (1)(2)(3)(4)(5)(6)(7)(8)(9)(10)

Saturday _____   **Goal Tasks**

    Schedual Notes
_____

_____

_____

_____

                          Productivity Score

Routine Tasks completed (1)(2)(3)(4)(5)(6)(7)(8)(9)(10)

Sunday _____   **Goal Tasks**

    Schedual Notes
_____

_____

_____

_____

                          Productivity Score

Routine Tasks completed (1)(2)(3)(4)(5)(6)(7)(8)(9)(10)

Weekly Reflection

Weekly wins; What went well?

What routine tasks or goal tasks were not completed and why?

What have you learned? What would you change?

Month: _____

	Sunday	Monday	Tuesday	Wednesday	Thursday	Friday	Saturday

Monthly Goals

Goal   Tasks

Goal   Tasks

Goal   Tasks

Monthly Goals

Goal

Tasks

Goal

Tasks

Goal

Tasks

PHILIPPIANS 4:4
REJOICE IN THE LORD ALWAYS:
AND AGAIN I SAY, REJOICE.

$\mathcal{W}$eek: _____

Goal Tasks (order of priority)	Routine Tasks
_____	
_____	
_____	
_____	
_____	
_____	
_____	
_____	
_____	
_____	
_____	
_____	

Monday _____   **Goal Tasks**

    Schedual Notes   _____

                      _____

                      _____

                      _____

Productivity Score

Routine Tasks completed ① ② ③ ④ ⑤ ⑥ ⑦ ⑧ ⑨ ⑩

Tuesday _____   **Goal Tasks**

    Schedual Notes   _____

                      _____

                      _____

                      _____

Productivity Score

Routine Tasks completed ① ② ③ ④ ⑤ ⑥ ⑦ ⑧ ⑨ ⑩

Wednesday_____   **Goal Tasks**

    Schedual Notes   _____

                      _____

                      _____

                      _____

Productivity Score

Routine Tasks completed ① ② ③ ④ ⑤ ⑥ ⑦ ⑧ ⑨ ⑩

Thursday _____   **Goal Tasks**

    Schedual Notes   _____

                      _____

                      _____

                      _____

Productivity Score

Routine Tasks completed ① ② ③ ④ ⑤ ⑥ ⑦ ⑧ ⑨ ⑩

Friday _____   **Goal Tasks**

    Schedual Notes   _____

                      _____

                      _____

                      _____

                      Productivity Score

Routine Tasks completed ①②③④⑤⑥⑦⑧⑨⑩

Saturday _____   **Goal Tasks**

    Schedual Notes   _____

                      _____

                      _____

                      _____

                      Productivity Score

Routine Tasks completed ①②③④⑤⑥⑦⑧⑨⑩

Sunday _____   **Goal Tasks**

    Schedual Notes   _____

                      _____

                      _____

                      _____

                      Productivity Score

Routine Tasks completed ①②③④⑤⑥⑦⑧⑨⑩

Weekly Reflection

Weekly wins; What went well?

What routine tasks or goal tasks were not completed and why?

What have you learned? What would you change?

PHILIPPIANS 4:6
BE CAREFUL FOR NOTHING; BUT IN EVERY THING BY PRAYER AND SUPPLICATION WITH THANKSGIVING LET YOUR REQUESTS BE MADE KNOWN UNTO

Week: _____

Goal Tasks
(order of priority)

_____
_____
_____
_____
_____
_____
_____
_____
_____
_____
_____
_____
_____

Routine Tasks

Monday _____

Schedual Notes

Goal Tasks

_____

_____

_____

_____

Productivity Score

Routine Tasks completed ①②③④⑤⑥⑦⑧⑨⑩

Tuesday _____

Schedual Notes

Goal Tasks

_____

_____

_____

_____

Productivity Score

Routine Tasks completed ①②③④⑤⑥⑦⑧⑨⑩

Wednesday_____

Schedual Notes

Goal Tasks

_____

_____

_____

_____

Productivity Score

Routine Tasks completed ①②③④⑤⑥⑦⑧⑨⑩

Thursday _____

Schedual Notes

Goal Tasks

_____

_____

_____

_____

Productivity Score

Routine Tasks completed ①②③④⑤⑥⑦⑧⑨⑩

Friday _____ **Goal Tasks**

    Schedual Notes

_____

_____

_____

_____

Productivity Score

Routine Tasks completed ① ② ③ ④ ⑤ ⑥ ⑦ ⑧ ⑨ ⑩

Saturday _____ **Goal Tasks**

    Schedual Notes

_____

_____

_____

_____

Productivity Score

Routine Tasks completed ① ② ③ ④ ⑤ ⑥ ⑦ ⑧ ⑨ ⑩

Sunday _____ **Goal Tasks**

    Schedual Notes

_____

_____

_____

_____

Productivity Score

Routine Tasks completed ① ② ③ ④ ⑤ ⑥ ⑦ ⑧ ⑨ ⑩

Weekly Reflection

Weekly wins; What went well?

What routine tasks or goal tasks were not completed and why?

What have you learned? What would you change?

PHILIPPIANS 4:7
AND THE PEACE OF GOD, WHICH PASSETH ALL UNDERSTANDING, SHALL KEEP YOUR HEARTS AND MINDS THROUGH CHRIST JESUS.

Week: _____

Goal Tasks
(order of priority)

Routine Tasks

_____

_____

_____

_____

_____

_____

_____

_____

_____

_____

_____

_____

_____

Monday _____   **Goal Tasks**

    Schedual Notes

_____

_____

_____

_____

Productivity Score

Routine Tasks completed ①②③④⑤⑥⑦⑧⑨⑩

Tuesday _____   **Goal Tasks**

    Schedual Notes

_____

_____

_____

_____

Productivity Score

Routine Tasks completed ①②③④⑤⑥⑦⑧⑨⑩

Wednesday _____   **Goal Tasks**

    Schedual Notes

_____

_____

_____

_____

Productivity Score

Routine Tasks completed ①②③④⑤⑥⑦⑧⑨⑩

Thursday _____   **Goal Tasks**

    Schedual Notes

_____

_____

_____

_____

Productivity Score

Routine Tasks completed ①②③④⑤⑥⑦⑧⑨⑩

Friday _____   **Goal Tasks**

   Schedual Notes   _____
                                   _____
                                   _____
                                   _____

                                   Productivity Score

Routine Tasks completed ① ② ③ ④ ⑤ ⑥ ⑦ ⑧ ⑨ ⑩

Saturday _____   **Goal Tasks**

   Schedual Notes   _____
                                   _____
                                   _____
                                   _____

                                   Productivity Score

Routine Tasks completed ① ② ③ ④ ⑤ ⑥ ⑦ ⑧ ⑨ ⑩

Sunday _____   **Goal Tasks**

   Schedual Notes   _____
                                   _____
                                   _____
                                   _____

                                   Productivity Score

Routine Tasks completed ① ② ③ ④ ⑤ ⑥ ⑦ ⑧ ⑨ ⑩

Weekly Reflection

Weekly wins; What went well?

What routine tasks or goal tasks were not completed and why?

What have you learned? What would you change?

PHILIPPIANS 4:8

FINALLY, BRETHREN, WHATSOEVER THINGS ARE TRUE, WHATSOE-
VER THINGS ARE HONEST, WHATSOEVER THINGS ARE JUST, WHAT-
SOEVER THINGS ARE PURE, WHATSOEVER THINGS ARE LOVELY,
WHATSOEVER THINGS ARE OF GOOD REPORT; IF THERE BE ANY
VIRTUE, AND IF THERE BE ANY PRAISE, THINK ON THESE THINGS

Week: _____

Goal Tasks (order of priority)	Routine Tasks
_____	
_____	
_____	
_____	
_____	
_____	
_____	
_____	
_____	
_____	
_____	
_____	
_____	

Monday _____

Schedual Notes

Goal Tasks

_____
_____
_____
_____

Productivity Score

Routine Tasks completed ①②③④⑤⑥⑦⑧⑨⑩

Tuesday _____

Schedual Notes

Goal Tasks

_____
_____
_____
_____

Productivity Score

Routine Tasks completed ①②③④⑤⑥⑦⑧⑨⑩

Wednesday_____

Schedual Notes

Goal Tasks

_____
_____
_____
_____

Productivity Score

Routine Tasks completed ①②③④⑤⑥⑦⑧⑨⑩

Thursday _____

Schedual Notes

Goal Tasks

_____
_____
_____
_____

Productivity Score

Routine Tasks completed ①②③④⑤⑥⑦⑧⑨⑩

Friday _____   **Goal Tasks**

Schedual Notes   _____
                                 _____
                                 _____
                                 _____

                                 Productivity Score

Routine Tasks completed ①②③④⑤⑥⑦⑧⑨⑩

Saturday _____   **Goal Tasks**

Schedual Notes   _____
                                 _____
                                 _____
                                 _____

                                 Productivity Score

Routine Tasks completed ①②③④⑤⑥⑦⑧⑨⑩

Sunday _____   **Goal Tasks**

Schedual Notes   _____
                                 _____
                                 _____
                                 _____

                                 Productivity Score

Routine Tasks completed ①②③④⑤⑥⑦⑧⑨⑩

Weekly Reflection

Weekly wins; What went well?

What routine tasks or goal tasks were not completed and why?

What have you learned? What would you change?

Month: _____

Sunday	Monday	Tuesday	Wednesday	Thursday	Friday	Saturday

Monthly Goals

Dream

Goal	Tasks

Dream

Goal	Tasks

Dream

Goal	Tasks

Monthly Goals

Goal

Tasks

Goal

Tasks

Goal

Tasks

PSALM 37:4
DELIGHT THYSELF ALSO IN THE LORD: AND HE SHALL GIVE THEE THE DESIRES OF THINE HEART.

Week: _____

Goal Tasks (order of priority)	Routine Tasks
_____	
_____	
_____	
_____	
_____	
_____	
_____	
_____	
_____	
_____	
_____	
_____	
_____	

Monday _____

Goal Tasks

Schedual Notes

_____

_____

_____

_____

Productivity Score

Routine Tasks completed ①②③④⑤⑥⑦⑧⑨⑩

Tuesday _____

Goal Tasks

Schedual Notes

_____

_____

_____

_____

Productivity Score

Routine Tasks completed ①②③④⑤⑥⑦⑧⑨⑩

Wednesday_____

Goal Tasks

Schedual Notes

_____

_____

_____

_____

Productivity Score

Routine Tasks completed ①②③④⑤⑥⑦⑧⑨⑩

Thursday _____

Goal Tasks

Schedual Notes

_____

_____

_____

_____

Productivity Score

Routine Tasks completed ①②③④⑤⑥⑦⑧⑨⑩

Friday _____   **Goal Tasks**

    Schedual Notes
                                            _____
                                            _____
                                            _____
                                            _____

Productivity Score

Routine Tasks completed ①②③④⑤⑥⑦⑧⑨⑩

Saturday _____   **Goal Tasks**

    Schedual Notes
                                            _____
                                          _____
                                            _____
                                            _____

Productivity Score

Routine Tasks completed ①②③④⑤⑥⑦⑧⑨⑩

Sunday _____   **Goal Tasks**

    Schedual Notes
                                            _____
                                          _____
                                          _____
                                          _____

Productivity Score

Routine Tasks completed ①②③④⑤⑥⑦⑧⑨⑩

Weekly Reflection

Weekly wins; What went well?

What routine tasks or goal tasks were not completed and why?

What have you learned? What would you change?

PROVERBS 3:5
TRUST IN THE LORD WITH ALL THINE HEART; AND LEAN NOT UNTO THINE OWN UNDERSTANDING.

Week: _____

Goal Tasks (order of priority)	Routine Tasks
_____	
_____	
_____	
_____	
_____	
_____	
_____	
_____	
_____	
_____	
_____	
_____	
_____	

Monday _____ **Goal Tasks**

    Schedual Notes
        _____

        _____

        _____

        _____

        Productivity Score

Routine Tasks completed (1)(2)(3)(4)(5)(6)(7)(8)(9)(10)

Tuesday _____ **Goal Tasks**

    Schedual Notes
        _____

        _____

        _____

        _____

        Productivity Score

Routine Tasks completed (1)(2)(3)(4)(5)(6)(7)(8)(9)(10)

Wednesday _____ **Goal Tasks**

    Schedual Notes
        _____

        _____

        _____

        _____

        Productivity Score

Routine Tasks completed (1)(2)(3)(4)(5)(6)(7)(8)(9)(10)

Thursday _____ **Goal Tasks**

    Schedual Notes
        _____

        _____

        _____

        _____

        Productivity Score

Routine Tasks completed (1)(2)(3)(4)(5)(6)(7)(8)(9)(10)

Friday _____

Schedual Notes

Goal Tasks

_____
_____
_____
_____

Productivity Score

Routine Tasks completed ①②③④⑤⑥⑦⑧⑨⑩

Saturday _____

Schedual Notes

Goal Tasks

_____
_____
_____
_____

Productivity Score

Routine Tasks completed ①②③④⑤⑥⑦⑧⑨⑩

Sunday _____

Schedual Notes

Goal Tasks

_____
_____
_____
_____

Productivity Score

Routine Tasks completed ①②③④⑤⑥⑦⑧⑨⑩

Weekly Reflection

Weekly wins; What went well?

What routine tasks or goal tasks were not completed and why?

What have you learned? What would you change?

PROVERBS 3:6
IN ALL THY WAYS ACKNOWLEDGE HIM, AND HE SHALL DIRECT THY PATHS.

Week: _____

Goal Tasks (order of priority)	Routine Tasks
_____	
_____	
_____	
_____	
_____	
_____	
_____	
_____	
_____	
_____	
_____	
_____	
_____	
_____	
_____	

Monday _____   **Goal Tasks**

    Schedual Notes
    _____

    _____

    _____

    _____

Productivity Score

Routine Tasks completed ① ② ③ ④ ⑤ ⑥ ⑦ ⑧ ⑨ ⑩

Tuesday _____   **Goal Tasks**

    Schedual Notes
    _____

    _____

    _____

    _____

Productivity Score

Routine Tasks completed ① ② ③ ④ ⑤ ⑥ ⑦ ⑧ ⑨ ⑩

Wednesday_____   **Goal Tasks**

    Schedual Notes
    _____

    _____

    _____

    _____

Productivity Score

Routine Tasks completed ① ② ③ ④ ⑤ ⑥ ⑦ ⑧ ⑨ ⑩

Thursday _____   **Goal Tasks**

    Schedual Notes
    _____

    _____

    _____

    _____

Productivity Score

Routine Tasks completed ① ② ③ ④ ⑤ ⑥ ⑦ ⑧ ⑨ ⑩

Friday _____   **Goal Tasks**

    Schedual Notes
_____
_____
_____
_____

    Productivity Score

Routine Tasks completed ① ② ③ ④ ⑤ ⑥ ⑦ ⑧ ⑨ ⑩

Saturday _____   **Goal Tasks**

    Schedual Notes
_____
_____
_____
_____

    Productivity Score

Routine Tasks completed ① ② ③ ④ ⑤ ⑥ ⑦ ⑧ ⑨ ⑩

Sunday _____   **Goal Tasks**

    Schedual Notes
_____
_____
_____
_____

    Productivity Score

Routine Tasks completed ① ② ③ ④ ⑤ ⑥ ⑦ ⑧ ⑨ ⑩

Weekly Reflection

Weekly wins; What went well?

What routine tasks or goal tasks were not completed and why?

What have you learned? What would you change?

2 Timothy 1:7
For God hath not given us the spirit of fear; but of power, and of love, and of a sound mind.

$\mathcal{W}$eek: _____

Goal Tasks (order of priority)	Routine Tasks
_____	
_____	
_____	
_____	
_____	
_____	
_____	
_____	
_____	
_____	
_____	
_____	

Monday _____   **Goal Tasks**

   Schedual Notes   _____
                                            _____
                                            _____
                                            _____

                                            Productivity Score

Routine Tasks completed ①②③④⑤⑥⑦⑧⑨⑩

Tuesday _____   **Goal Tasks**

   Schedual Notes   _____
                                            _____
                                            _____
                                            _____

                                            Productivity Score

Routine Tasks completed ①②③④⑤⑥⑦⑧⑨⑩

Wednesday_____   **Goal Tasks**

   Schedual Notes   _____
                                            _____
                                            _____
                                            _____

                                            Productivity Score

Routine Tasks completed ①②③④⑤⑥⑦⑧⑨⑩

Thursday _____   **Goal Tasks**

   Schedual Notes   _____
                                            _____
                                            _____
                                            _____

                                            Productivity Score

Routine Tasks completed ①②③④⑤⑥⑦⑧⑨⑩

Friday _____

Schedual Notes

Goal Tasks

_____
_____
_____
_____

Productivity Score

Routine Tasks completed ①②③④⑤⑥⑦⑧⑨⑩

Saturday _____

Schedual Notes

Goal Tasks

_____
_____
_____
_____

Productivity Score

Routine Tasks completed ①②③④⑤⑥⑦⑧⑨⑩

Sunday _____

Schedual Notes

Goal Tasks

_____
_____
_____
_____

Productivity Score

Routine Tasks completed ①②③④⑤⑥⑦⑧⑨⑩

Weekly Reflection

Weekly wins; What went well?

What routine tasks or goal tasks were not completed and why?

What have you learned? What would you change?

Month: _____

Sunday	Monday	Tuesday	Wednesday	Thursday	Friday	Saturday

Monthly Goals

Goal

Tasks

Goal

Tasks

Goal

Tasks

Monthly Goals

Goal

Tasks

Goal

Tasks

Goal

Tasks

PSALM 20:7
SOME TRUST IN CHARIOTS, AND SOME IN HORSES: BUT WE WILL REMEMBER THE NAME OF THE LORD OUR GOD.

Week: _____

Goal Tasks
(order of priority)

_____
_____
_____
_____
_____
_____
_____
_____
_____
_____
_____
_____
_____

Routine Tasks

Monday _____   **Goal Tasks**

    Schedual Notes   _____

_____

_____

_____

Productivity Score

Routine Tasks completed ①②③④⑤⑥⑦⑧⑨⑩

Tuesday _____   **Goal Tasks**

    Schedual Notes   _____

_____

_____

_____

Productivity Score

Routine Tasks completed ①②③④⑤⑥⑦⑧⑨⑩

Wednesday_____   **Goal Tasks**

    Schedual Notes   _____

_____

_____

_____

Productivity Score

Routine Tasks completed ①②③④⑤⑥⑦⑧⑨⑩

Thursday _____   **Goal Tasks**

    Schedual Notes   _____

_____

_____

_____

Productivity Score

Routine Tasks completed ①②③④⑤⑥⑦⑧⑨⑩

Friday _____   **Goal Tasks**

   Schedual Notes   _____
                                _____
                                _____
                                _____

                                Productivity Score

Routine Tasks completed ①②③④⑤⑥⑦⑧⑨⑩

Saturday _____   **Goal Tasks**

   Schedual Notes   _____
                                _____
                                _____
                                _____

                                Productivity Score

Routine Tasks completed ①②③④⑤⑥⑦⑧⑨⑩

Sunday _____   **Goal Tasks**

   Schedual Notes   _____
                                _____
                                _____
                                _____

                                Productivity Score

Routine Tasks completed ①②③④⑤⑥⑦⑧⑨⑩

Weekly Reflection

Weekly wins; What went well?

What routine tasks or goal tasks were not completed and why?

What have you learned? What would you change?

GENESIS 39:2
THE LORD WAS WITH JOSEPH, AND HE WAS A SUCCESSFUL MAN

Week: _____

Goal Tasks (order of priority)	Routine Tasks
_____	
_____	
_____	
_____	
_____	
_____	
_____	
_____	
_____	
_____	
_____	
_____	
_____	
_____	
_____	
_____	

Monday _____ **Goal Tasks**

Schedual Notes

_____

_____

_____

_____

Productivity Score

Routine Tasks completed ① ② ③ ④ ⑤ ⑥ ⑦ ⑧ ⑨ ⑩

Tuesday _____ **Goal Tasks**

Schedual Notes

_____

_____

_____

_____

Productivity Score

Routine Tasks completed ① ② ③ ④ ⑤ ⑥ ⑦ ⑧ ⑨ ⑩

Wednesday_____ **Goal Tasks**

Schedual Notes

_____

_____

_____

_____

Productivity Score

Routine Tasks completed ① ② ③ ④ ⑤ ⑥ ⑦ ⑧ ⑨ ⑩

Thursday _____ **Goal Tasks**

Schedual Notes

_____

_____

_____

_____

Productivity Score

Routine Tasks completed ① ② ③ ④ ⑤ ⑥ ⑦ ⑧ ⑨ ⑩

Friday _____   **Goal Tasks**

    Schedual Notes

Routine Tasks completed

Productivity Score

① ② ③ ④ ⑤ ⑥ ⑦ ⑧ ⑨ ⑩

Saturday _____   **Goal Tasks**

    Schedual Notes

Productivity Score

Routine Tasks completed   ① ② ③ ④ ⑤ ⑥ ⑦ ⑧ ⑨ ⑩

Sunday _____   **Goal Tasks**

    Schedual Notes

Productivity Score

Routine Tasks completed   ① ② ③ ④ ⑤ ⑥ ⑦ ⑧ ⑨ ⑩

Weekly Reflection

Weekly wins; What went well?

What routine tasks or goal tasks were not completed and why?

What have you learned? What would you change?

PSALM 1:3
AND HE SHALL BE LIKE A TREE PLANTED BY THE RIVERS OF WATER, THAT BRINGETH FORTH HIS FRUIT IN HIS SEASON; HIS LEAF ALSO SHALL NOT WITHER; AND WHATSOEVER HE DOETH SHALL PROSPER.

$\mathcal{W}$eek: _____

Goal Tasks (order of priority)	Routine Tasks
_____	
_____	
_____	
_____	
_____	
_____	
_____	
_____	
_____	
_____	
_____	
_____	
_____	
_____	

Monday _____   **Goal Tasks**

   Schedual Notes

                                         Productivity Score

Routine Tasks completed ① ② ③ ④ ⑤ ⑥ ⑦ ⑧ ⑨ ⑩

Tuesday _____   **Goal Tasks**

   Schedual Notes

                                         Productivity Score

Routine Tasks completed ① ② ③ ④ ⑤ ⑥ ⑦ ⑧ ⑨ ⑩

Wednesday_____   **Goal Tasks**

   Schedual Notes

                                         Productivity Score

Routine Tasks completed ① ② ③ ④ ⑤ ⑥ ⑦ ⑧ ⑨ ⑩

Thursday _____   **Goal Tasks**

   Schedual Notes

                                         Productivity Score

Routine Tasks completed ① ② ③ ④ ⑤ ⑥ ⑦ ⑧ ⑨ ⑩

Friday _____

Schedual Notes

Goal Tasks

_____
_____
_____
_____

Productivity Score

Routine Tasks completed ①②③④⑤⑥⑦⑧⑨⑩

Saturday _____

Schedual Notes

Goal Tasks

_____
_____
_____
_____

Productivity Score

Routine Tasks completed ①②③④⑤⑥⑦⑧⑨⑩

Sunday _____

Schedual Notes

Goal Tasks

_____
_____
_____
_____

Productivity Score

Routine Tasks completed ①②③④⑤⑥⑦⑧⑨⑩

Weekly Reflection

Weekly wins; What went well?

What routine tasks or goal tasks were not completed and why?

What have you learned? What would you change?

Proverbs 16:3
Commit your work to the LORD, and your plans will be established.

Week: _____

Goal Tasks (order of priority)	Routine Tasks
_____	
_____	
_____	
_____	
_____	
_____	
_____	
_____	
_____	
_____	
_____	
_____	
_____	
_____	

Monday _____   **Goal Tasks**

   Schedual Notes   _____
                                    _____
                                    _____
                                    _____

                                    Productivity Score

Routine Tasks completed ①②③④⑤⑥⑦⑧⑨⑩

Tuesday _____   **Goal Tasks**

   Schedual Notes   _____
                                    _____
                                    _____
                                    _____

                                    Productivity Score

Routine Tasks completed ①②③④⑤⑥⑦⑧⑨⑩

Wednesday_____   **Goal Tasks**

   Schedual Notes   _____
                                    _____
                                    _____
                                    _____

                                    Productivity Score

Routine Tasks completed ①②③④⑤⑥⑦⑧⑨⑩

Thursday _____   **Goal Tasks**

   Schedual Notes   _____
                                    _____
                                    _____
                                    _____

                                    Productivity Score

Routine Tasks completed ①②③④⑤⑥⑦⑧⑨⑩

Friday _____   **Goal Tasks**

    Schedual Notes   _____
                                                  _____
                                                  _____
                                                  _____

                                                  Productivity Score
Routine Tasks completed ①②③④⑤⑥⑦⑧⑨⑩

Saturday _____   **Goal Tasks**

    Schedual Notes   _____
                                                  _____
                                                  _____
                                                  _____

                                                  Productivity Score
Routine Tasks completed ①②③④⑤⑥⑦⑧⑨⑩

Sunday _____   **Goal Tasks**

    Schedual Notes   _____
                                                  _____
                                                  _____
                                                  _____

                                                  Productivity Score
Routine Tasks completed ①②③④⑤⑥⑦⑧⑨⑩

Weekly Reflection

Weekly wins; What went well?

What routine tasks or goal tasks were not completed and why?

What have you learned? What would you change?

Month: _____

Sunday	Monday	Tuesday	Wednesday	Thursday	Friday	Saturday

Monthly Goals

Goal

Tasks

Goal

Tasks

Goal

Tasks

Monthly Goals

Goal

Tasks

Goal

Tasks

Goal

Tasks

PHILIPPIANS 1:6
AND I AM SURE OF THIS, THAT HE WHO BEGAN A GOOD WORK IN YOU WILL BRING IT TO COMPLETION UNTO THE DAY OF CHRIST.

Week: _____

Goal Tasks
(order of priority)

_____
_____
_____
_____
_____
_____
_____
_____
_____
_____
_____
_____
_____
_____

Routine Tasks

Monday _____

Schedual Notes

Goal Tasks

_____
_____
_____
_____

Productivity Score

Routine Tasks completed ①②③④⑤⑥⑦⑧⑨⑩

Tuesday _____

Schedual Notes

Goal Tasks

_____
_____
_____
_____

Productivity Score

Routine Tasks completed ①②③④⑤⑥⑦⑧⑨⑩

Wednesday _____

Schedual Notes

Goal Tasks

_____
_____
_____
_____

Productivity Score

Routine Tasks completed ①②③④⑤⑥⑦⑧⑨⑩

Thursday _____

Schedual Notes

Goal Tasks

_____
_____
_____
_____

Productivity Score

Routine Tasks completed ①②③④⑤⑥⑦⑧⑨⑩

Friday _____   **Goal Tasks**

   Schedual Notes   _____
_____
_____
_____

Productivity Score

Routine Tasks completed ① ② ③ ④ ⑤ ⑥ ⑦ ⑧ ⑨ ⑩

Saturday _____   **Goal Tasks**

   Schedual Notes   _____
_____
_____
_____

Productivity Score

Routine Tasks completed ① ② ③ ④ ⑤ ⑥ ⑦ ⑧ ⑨ ⑩

Sunday _____   **Goal Tasks**

   Schedual Notes   _____
_____
_____
_____

Productivity Score

Routine Tasks completed ① ② ③ ④ ⑤ ⑥ ⑦ ⑧ ⑨ ⑩

Weekly Reflection

Weekly wins; What went well?

What routine tasks or goal tasks were not completed and why?

What have you learned? What would you change?

ISAIAH 41:10

FEAR NOT, FOR I AM WITH YOU; BE NOT DISMAYED, FOR I AM YOUR GOD; I WILL STRENGTHEN YOU, I WILL HELP YOU, I WILL UPHOLD YOU WITH MY RIGHTEOUS RIGHT HAND.

Week: _____

Goal Tasks (order of priority)	Routine Tasks
_____	
_____	
_____	
_____	
_____	
_____	
_____	
_____	
_____	
_____	
_____	
_____	
_____	
_____	

Monday _____ **Goal Tasks**

    Schedual Notes   _____

                        _____

                        _____

                        _____

                        Productivity Score

Routine Tasks completed ① ② ③ ④ ⑤ ⑥ ⑦ ⑧ ⑨ ⑩

Tuesday _____ **Goal Tasks**

    Schedual Notes   _____

                        _____

                        _____

                        _____

                        Productivity Score

Routine Tasks completed ① ② ③ ④ ⑤ ⑥ ⑦ ⑧ ⑨ ⑩

Wednesday_____ **Goal Tasks**

    Schedual Notes   _____

                        _____

                        _____

                        _____

                        Productivity Score

Routine Tasks completed ① ② ③ ④ ⑤ ⑥ ⑦ ⑧ ⑨ ⑩

Thursday _____ **Goal Tasks**

    Schedual Notes   _____

                        _____

                        _____

                        _____

                        Productivity Score

Routine Tasks completed ① ② ③ ④ ⑤ ⑥ ⑦ ⑧ ⑨ ⑩

Friday _____

    Schedual Notes

Goal Tasks

_____

_____

_____

_____

Productivity Score

Routine Tasks completed ① ② ③ ④ ⑤ ⑥ ⑦ ⑧ ⑨ ⑩

Saturday _____

    Schedual Notes

Goal Tasks

_____

_____

_____

_____

Productivity Score

Routine Tasks completed ① ② ③ ④ ⑤ ⑥ ⑦ ⑧ ⑨ ⑩

Sunday _____

    Schedual Notes

Goal Tasks

_____

_____

_____

_____

Productivity Score

Routine Tasks completed ① ② ③ ④ ⑤ ⑥ ⑦ ⑧ ⑨ ⑩

Weekly Reflection

Weekly wins; What went well?

What routine tasks or goal tasks were not completed and why?

What have you learned? What would you change?

PSALM 1:3
AND HE SHALL BE LIKE A TREE PLANTED BY THE RIVERS OF WATER, THAT BRINGETH FORTH HIS FRUIT IN HIS SEASON; HIS LEAF ALSO SHALL NOT WITHER; AND WHATSOEVER HE DOETH SHALL PROSPER.

Week: _____

Goal Tasks (order of priority)	Routine Tasks
_____	
_____	
_____	
_____	
_____	
_____	
_____	
_____	
_____	
_____	
_____	
_____	
_____	
_____	

Monday _____

Goal Tasks

Schedual Notes

_____

_____

_____

_____

Productivity Score

Routine Tasks completed   ① ② ③ ④ ⑤ ⑥ ⑦ ⑧ ⑨ ⑩

Tuesday _____

Goal Tasks

Schedual Notes

_____

_____

_____

_____

Productivity Score

Routine Tasks completed   ① ② ③ ④ ⑤ ⑥ ⑦ ⑧ ⑨ ⑩

Wednesday _____

Goal Tasks

Schedual Notes

_____

_____

_____

_____

Productivity Score

Routine Tasks completed   ① ② ③ ④ ⑤ ⑥ ⑦ ⑧ ⑨ ⑩

Thursday _____

Goal Tasks

Schedual Notes

_____

_____

_____

_____

Productivity Score

Routine Tasks completed   ① ② ③ ④ ⑤ ⑥ ⑦ ⑧ ⑨ ⑩

Friday _____   **Goal Tasks**

    Schedual Notes   _____
                               _____
                               _____
                               _____

                               Productivity Score

Routine Tasks completed ① ② ③ ④ ⑤ ⑥ ⑦ ⑧ ⑨ ⑩

Saturday _____   **Goal Tasks**

    Schedual Notes   _____
                               _____
                               _____
                               _____

                               Productivity Score

Routine Tasks completed ① ② ③ ④ ⑤ ⑥ ⑦ ⑧ ⑨ ⑩

Sunday _____   **Goal Tasks**

    Schedual Notes   _____
                               _____
                               _____
                               _____

                               Productivity Score

Routine Tasks completed ① ② ③ ④ ⑤ ⑥ ⑦ ⑧ ⑨ ⑩

Weekly Reflection

Weekly wins; What went well?

What routine tasks or goal tasks were not completed and why?

What have you learned? What would you change?

Habakkuk 2:2
And the LORD answered me, and said, Write the vision, and make it plain upon tables, that he may run

Week: _____

Goal Tasks (order of priority)	Routine Tasks
_____	
_____	
_____	
_____	
_____	
_____	
_____	
_____	
_____	
_____	
_____	
_____	

Monday _____   **Goal Tasks**

    Schedual Notes   _____
                                         _____
                                         _____
                                         _____

                                         Productivity Score

Routine Tasks completed ①②③④⑤⑥⑦⑧⑨⑩

Tuesday _____   **Goal Tasks**

    Schedual Notes   _____
                                         _____
                                         _____
                                         _____

                                         Productivity Score

Routine Tasks completed ①②③④⑤⑥⑦⑧⑨⑩

Wednesday _____   **Goal Tasks**

    Schedual Notes   _____
                                         _____
                                         _____
                                         _____

                                         Productivity Score

Routine Tasks completed ①②③④⑤⑥⑦⑧⑨⑩

Thursday _____   **Goal Tasks**

    Schedual Notes   _____
                                         _____
                                         _____
                                         _____

                                         Productivity Score

Routine Tasks completed ①②③④⑤⑥⑦⑧⑨⑩

Friday _____

Schedual Notes

Goal Tasks

_____
_____
_____
_____

Productivity Score

Routine Tasks completed ①②③④⑤⑥⑦⑧⑨⑩

Saturday _____

Schedual Notes

Goal Tasks

_____
_____
_____
_____

Productivity Score

Routine Tasks completed ①②③④⑤⑥⑦⑧⑨⑩

Sunday _____

Schedual Notes

Goal Tasks

_____
_____
_____
_____

Productivity Score

Routine Tasks completed ①②③④⑤⑥⑦⑧⑨⑩

Weekly Reflection

Weekly wins; What went well?

What routine tasks or goal tasks were not completed and why?

What have you learned? What would you change?

Month: _____

Sunday	Monday	Tuesday	Wednesday	Thursday	Friday	Saturday

Monthly Goals

Goal

Tasks

Goal

Tasks

Goal

Tasks

Monthly Goals

Dream

Goal   Tasks

Dream

Goal   Tasks

Dream

Goal   Tasks

ISAIAH 58:11
AND THE LORD SHALL GUIDE THEE CONTINUALLY, AND SATISFY THY SOUL IN DROUGHT, AND MAKE FAT THY BONES: AND THOU SHALT BE LIKE A WATERED GARDEN, AND LIKE A SPRING OF WATER, WHOSE WATERS FAIL NOT.

Week: _____

Goal Tasks (order of priority)	Routine Tasks
_____	
_____	
_____	
_____	
_____	
_____	
_____	
_____	
_____	
_____	
_____	
_____	
_____	
_____	

Monday _____ **Goal Tasks**

    Schedual Notes

_____

_____

_____

_____

Productivity Score

Routine Tasks completed ①②③④⑤⑥⑦⑧⑨⑩

Tuesday _____ **Goal Tasks**

    Schedual Notes

_____

_____

_____

_____

Productivity Score

Routine Tasks completed ①②③④⑤⑥⑦⑧⑨⑩

Wednesday _____ **Goal Tasks**

    Schedual Notes

_____

_____

_____

_____

Productivity Score

Routine Tasks completed ①②③④⑤⑥⑦⑧⑨⑩

Thursday _____ **Goal Tasks**

    Schedual Notes

_____

_____

_____

_____

Productivity Score

Routine Tasks completed ①②③④⑤⑥⑦⑧⑨⑩

Friday _____ **Goal Tasks**

Schedual Notes

_____

_____

_____

_____

Productivity Score

Routine Tasks completed ①②③④⑤⑥⑦⑧⑨⑩

Saturday _____ **Goal Tasks**

Schedual Notes

_____

_____

_____

_____

Productivity Score

Routine Tasks completed ①②③④⑤⑥⑦⑧⑨⑩

Sunday _____ **Goal Tasks**

Schedual Notes

_____

_____

_____

_____

Productivity Score

Routine Tasks completed ①②③④⑤⑥⑦⑧⑨⑩

Weekly Reflection

Weekly wins; What went well?

What routine tasks or goal tasks were not completed and why?

What have you learned? What would you change?

PSALM 5:12
FOR THOU, LORD, WILT BLESS THE RIGHTEOUS; WITH FAVOUR WILT THOU COMPASS HIM AS WITH A SHIELD.

Week: _____

Goal Tasks
(order of priority)

_____
_____
_____
_____
_____
_____
_____
_____
_____
_____
_____
_____
_____

Routine Tasks

Monday _____   **Goal Tasks**

    Schedual Notes   _____

_____

_____

_____

Productivity Score

Routine Tasks completed ①②③④⑤⑥⑦⑧⑨⑩

Tuesday _____   **Goal Tasks**

    Schedual Notes   _____

_____

_____

_____

Productivity Score

Routine Tasks completed ①②③④⑤⑥⑦⑧⑨⑩

Wednesday _____   **Goal Tasks**

    Schedual Notes   _____

_____

_____

_____

Productivity Score

Routine Tasks completed ①②③④⑤⑥⑦⑧⑨⑩

Thursday _____   **Goal Tasks**

    Schedual Notes   _____

_____

_____

_____

Productivity Score

    Routine Tasks completed ①②③④⑤⑥⑦⑧⑨⑩

Friday _____ **Goal Tasks**

Schedual Notes

_____

_____

_____

_____

Productivity Score

Routine Tasks completed ① ② ③ ④ ⑤ ⑥ ⑦ ⑧ ⑨ ⑩

Saturday _____ **Goal Tasks**

Schedual Notes

_____

_____

_____

_____

Productivity Score

Routine Tasks completed ① ② ③ ④ ⑤ ⑥ ⑦ ⑧ ⑨ ⑩

Sunday _____ **Goal Tasks**

Schedual Notes

_____

_____

_____

_____

Productivity Score

Routine Tasks completed ① ② ③ ④ ⑤ ⑥ ⑦ ⑧ ⑨ ⑩

Weekly Reflection

Weekly wins; What went well?

What routine tasks or goal tasks were not completed and why?

What have you learned? What would you change?

DEUTERONOMY 8:18
BUT THOU SHALT REMEMBER THE LORD THY GOD: FOR IT IS
HE THAT GIVETH THEE POWER TO GET WEALTH, THAT HE MAY
ESTABLISH HIS COVENANT WHICH HE SWARE UNTO THY
FATHERS, AS IT IS THIS DAY.

Week: _____

Goal Tasks (order of priority)	Routine Tasks
_____	
_____	
_____	
_____	
_____	
_____	
_____	
_____	
_____	
_____	
_____	
_____	

Monday _____ **Goal Tasks**

Schedual Notes
_____
_____
_____
_____

Productivity Score

Routine Tasks completed ①②③④⑤⑥⑦⑧⑨⑩

Tuesday _____ **Goal Tasks**

Schedual Notes
_____
_____
_____
_____

Productivity Score

Routine Tasks completed ①②③④⑤⑥⑦⑧⑨⑩

Wednesday_____ **Goal Tasks**

Schedual Notes
_____
_____
_____
_____

Productivity Score

Routine Tasks completed ①②③④⑤⑥⑦⑧⑨⑩

Thursday _____ **Goal Tasks**

Schedual Notes
_____
_____
_____
_____

Productivity Score

Routine Tasks completed ①②③④⑤⑥⑦⑧⑨⑩

Friday _____

Schedual Notes

Routine Tasks completed

Saturday _____

Schedual Notes

Routine Tasks completed

Sunday _____

Schedual Notes

Routine Tasks completed

Goal Tasks
_____
_____
_____
_____

Productivity Score
①②③④⑤⑥⑦⑧⑨⑩

Goal Tasks
_____
_____
_____
_____

Productivity Score
①②③④⑤⑥⑦⑧⑨⑩

Goal Tasks
_____
_____
_____
_____

Productivity Score
①②③④⑤⑥⑦⑧⑨⑩

Weekly Reflection

Weekly wins; What went well?

What routine tasks or goal tasks were not completed and why?

What have you learned? What would you change?

DEUTERONOMY 30:9

THE LORD YOUR GOD WILL MAKE YOU ABUNDANTLY PROSPEROUS IN ALL
THE WORK OF YOUR HAND, IN THE FRUIT OF YOUR WOMB AND IN THE
FRUIT OF YOUR CATTLE AND IN THE FRUIT OF YOUR GROUND. FOR THE
LORD WILL AGAIN TAKE DELIGHT IN PROSPERING YOU, AS HE TOOK

Week: _____

Goal Tasks
(order of priority)

_____
_____
_____
_____
_____
_____
_____
_____
_____
_____
_____
_____
_____
_____

Routine Tasks

Monday _____ **Goal Tasks**

Schedual Notes
_____
_____
_____
_____

Productivity Score

Routine Tasks completed ①②③④⑤⑥⑦⑧⑨⑩

Tuesday _____ **Goal Tasks**

Schedual Notes
_____
_____
_____
_____

Productivity Score

Routine Tasks completed ①②③④⑤⑥⑦⑧⑨⑩

Wednesday _____ **Goal Tasks**

Schedual Notes
_____
_____
_____
_____

Productivity Score

Routine Tasks completed ①②③④⑤⑥⑦⑧⑨⑩

Thursday _____ **Goal Tasks**

Schedual Notes
_____
_____
_____
_____

Productivity Score

Routine Tasks completed ①②③④⑤⑥⑦⑧⑨⑩

Friday _____   **Goal Tasks**

    Schedual Notes   _____
                                 _____
                                 _____
                                 _____

                           Productivity Score

Routine Tasks completed ①②③④⑤⑥⑦⑧⑨⑩

Saturday _____   **Goal Tasks**

    Schedual Notes   _____
                                 _____
                                 _____
                                 _____

                           Productivity Score

Routine Tasks completed ①②③④⑤⑥⑦⑧⑨⑩

Sunday _____   **Goal Tasks**

    Schedual Notes   _____
                                 _____
                                 _____
                                 _____

                           Productivity Score

Routine Tasks completed ①②③④⑤⑥⑦⑧⑨⑩

Weekly Reflection

Weekly wins; What went well?

What routine tasks or goal tasks were not completed and why?

What have you learned? What would you change?

Month: _____

Sunday	Monday	Tuesday	Wednesday	Thursday	Friday	Saturday

Monthly Goals

Dream

Goal

Tasks

Dream

Goal

Tasks

Dream

Goal

Tasks

Monthly Goals

Dream

Goal   Tasks

Dream

Goal   Tasks

Dream

Goal   Tasks

MATTHEW 6:33
BUT SEEK FIRST THE KINGDOM OF GOD AND HIS RIGHTEOUS- NESS, AND ALL THESE THINGS WILL BE ADDED TO YOU.

Week: _____

Goal Tasks (order of priority)	Routine Tasks
_____	
_____	
_____	
_____	
_____	
_____	
_____	
_____	
_____	
_____	
_____	
_____	
_____	
_____	

Monday _____ **Goal Tasks**

   Schedual Notes
_____

_____

_____

_____

Productivity Score

Routine Tasks completed ①②③④⑤⑥⑦⑧⑨⑩

Tuesday _____ **Goal Tasks**

   Schedual Notes
_____

_____

_____

_____

Productivity Score

Routine Tasks completed ①②③④⑤⑥⑦⑧⑨⑩

Wednesday _____ **Goal Tasks**

   Schedual Notes
_____

_____

_____

_____

Productivity Score

Routine Tasks completed ①②③④⑤⑥⑦⑧⑨⑩

Thursday _____ **Goal Tasks**

   Schedual Notes
_____

_____

_____

_____

Productivity Score

Routine Tasks completed ①②③④⑤⑥⑦⑧⑨⑩

Friday _____ **Goal Tasks**

    Schedual Notes
_____
_____
_____
_____

Productivity Score

Routine Tasks completed ①②③④⑤⑥⑦⑧⑨⑩

Saturday _____ **Goal Tasks**

    Schedual Notes
_____
_____
_____
_____

Productivity Score

Routine Tasks completed ①②③④⑤⑥⑦⑧⑨⑩

Sunday _____ **Goal Tasks**

    Schedual Notes
_____
_____
_____
_____

Productivity Score

Routine Tasks completed ①②③④⑤⑥⑦⑧⑨⑩

Weekly Reflection

Weekly wins; What went well?

What routine tasks or goal tasks were not completed and why?

What have you learned? What would you change?

ISAIAH 55:11

SO SHALL MY WORD BE THAT GOES OUT FROM MY MOUTH; IT SHALL NOT RETURN TO ME EMPTY, BUT IT SHALL ACCOMPLISH THAT WHICH I PURPOSE, AND SHALL SUCCEED IN THE THING FOR WHICH I SENT IT.

Week: _____

Goal Tasks (order of priority)	Routine Tasks
_____	
_____	
_____	
_____	
_____	
_____	
_____	
_____	
_____	
_____	
_____	
_____	
_____	
_____	

Monday _____ **Goal Tasks**

    Schedual Notes
        _____
        _____
        _____
        _____

Productivity Score

Routine Tasks completed ① ② ③ ④ ⑤ ⑥ ⑦ ⑧ ⑨ ⑩

Tuesday _____ **Goal Tasks**

    Schedual Notes
        _____
        _____
        _____
        _____

Productivity Score

Routine Tasks completed ① ② ③ ④ ⑤ ⑥ ⑦ ⑧ ⑨ ⑩

Wednesday _____ **Goal Tasks**

    Schedual Notes
        _____
        _____
        _____
        _____

Productivity Score

Routine Tasks completed ① ② ③ ④ ⑤ ⑥ ⑦ ⑧ ⑨ ⑩

Thursday _____ **Goal Tasks**

    Schedual Notes
        _____
        _____
        _____
        _____

Productivity Score

Routine Tasks completed ① ② ③ ④ ⑤ ⑥ ⑦ ⑧ ⑨ ⑩

Friday _____

Goal Tasks

Schedual Notes

_____
_____
_____
_____

Productivity Score

Routine Tasks completed ① ② ③ ④ ⑤ ⑥ ⑦ ⑧ ⑨ ⑩

Saturday _____

Goal Tasks

Schedual Notes

_____
_____
_____
_____

Productivity Score

Routine Tasks completed ① ② ③ ④ ⑤ ⑥ ⑦ ⑧ ⑨ ⑩

Sunday _____

Goal Tasks

Schedual Notes

_____
_____
_____
_____

Productivity Score

Routine Tasks completed ① ② ③ ④ ⑤ ⑥ ⑦ ⑧ ⑨ ⑩

Weekly Reflection

Weekly wins; What went well?

What routine tasks or goal tasks were not completed and why?

What have you learned? What would you change?

MATTHEW 16:26

FOR WHAT IS A MAN PROFITED, IF HE SHALL GAIN THE WHOLE WORLD, AND LOSE HIS OWN SOUL? OR WHAT SHALL A MAN GIVE IN EXCHANGE FOR HIS SOUL?

Week: ______________________

Goal Tasks
(order of priority)

Routine Tasks

Monday _____   **Goal Tasks**

   Schedual Notes   _____

_____

_____

_____

Productivity Score

Routine Tasks completed ①②③④⑤⑥⑦⑧⑨⑩

Tuesday _____   **Goal Tasks**

   Schedual Notes   _____

_____

_____

_____

Productivity Score

Routine Tasks completed ①②③④⑤⑥⑦⑧⑨⑩

Wednesday_____   **Goal Tasks**

   Schedual Notes   _____

_____

_____

_____

Productivity Score

Routine Tasks completed ①②③④⑤⑥⑦⑧⑨⑩

Thursday _____   **Goal Tasks**

   Schedual Notes   _____

_____

_____

_____

Productivity Score

Routine Tasks completed ①②③④⑤⑥⑦⑧⑨⑩

Friday _____   **Goal Tasks**

    Schedual Notes   _____

                         _____

                         _____

                         _____

                     Productivity Score

Routine Tasks completed (1)(2)(3)(4)(5)(6)(7)(8)(9)(10)

Saturday _____   **Goal Tasks**

    Schedual Notes   _____

                         _____

                         _____

                         _____

                     Productivity Score

Routine Tasks completed (1)(2)(3)(4)(5)(6)(7)(8)(9)(10)

Sunday _____   **Goal Tasks**

    Schedual Notes   _____

                         _____

                         _____

                         _____

                     Productivity Score

Routine Tasks completed (1)(2)(3)(4)(5)(6)(7)(8)(9)(10)

Weekly Reflection

Weekly wins; What went well?

What routine tasks or goal tasks were not completed and why?

What have you learned? What would you change?

PROVERBS 10:4
LAZY HANDS MAKE FOR POVERTY, BUT DILIGENT HANDS BRING WEALTH.

Week: _____

Goal Tasks
(order of priority)

Routine Tasks

_____
_____
_____
_____
_____
_____
_____
_____
_____
_____
_____
_____
_____
_____

Monday _____ **Goal Tasks**

    Schedual Notes

                                  Productivity Score

Routine Tasks completed ①②③④⑤⑥⑦⑧⑨⑩

Tuesday _____ **Goal Tasks**

    Schedual Notes

                                  Productivity Score

Routine Tasks completed ①②③④⑤⑥⑦⑧⑨⑩

Wednesday_____ **Goal Tasks**

    Schedual Notes

                                  Productivity Score

Routine Tasks completed ①②③④⑤⑥⑦⑧⑨⑩

Thursday _____ **Goal Tasks**

    Schedual Notes

                                  Productivity Score

Routine Tasks completed ①②③④⑤⑥⑦⑧⑨⑩

Friday _____ **Goal Tasks**

Schedual Notes
_____
_____
_____
_____

Productivity Score

Routine Tasks completed ①②③④⑤⑥⑦⑧⑨⑩

Saturday _____ **Goal Tasks**

Schedual Notes
_____
_____
_____
_____

Productivity Score

Routine Tasks completed ①②③④⑤⑥⑦⑧⑨⑩

Sunday _____ **Goal Tasks**

Schedual Notes
_____
_____
_____
_____

Productivity Score

Routine Tasks completed ①②③④⑤⑥⑦⑧⑨⑩

Weekly Reflection

Weekly wins; What went well?

What routine tasks or goal tasks were not completed and why?

What have you learned? What would you change?

Month: _____

Sunday	Monday	Tuesday	Wednesday	Thursday	Friday	Saturday

Monthly Goals

Goal

Tasks

_____
_____

_____
_____
_____
_____
_____
_____

Goal

Tasks

_____
_____

_____
_____
_____
_____
_____

Goal

Tasks

_____
_____

_____
_____
_____
_____

Monthly Goals

Dream

_____

_____

Goal	Tasks
	_____
	_____
	_____
	_____
	_____

Dream

_____

_____

Goal	Tasks
	_____
	_____
	_____
	_____
	_____

Dream

_____

_____

Goal	Tasks
	_____
	_____
	_____
	_____

PROVERBS 10:22
THE BLESSING OF THE LORD MAKES RICH,
AND HE ADDS NO SORROW WITH IT.

Week: _____

Goal Tasks
(order of priority)

Routine Tasks

_____

_____

_____

_____

_____

_____

_____

_____

_____

_____

_____

_____

_____

_____

Monday _____

Goal Tasks

Schedual Notes

_____
_____
_____
_____

Productivity Score

Routine Tasks completed ①②③④⑤⑥⑦⑧⑨⑩

Tuesday _____

Goal Tasks

Schedual Notes

_____
_____
_____
_____

Productivity Score

Routine Tasks completed ①②③④⑤⑥⑦⑧⑨⑩

Wednesday_____

Goal Tasks

Schedual Notes

_____
_____
_____
_____

Productivity Score

Routine Tasks completed ①②③④⑤⑥⑦⑧⑨⑩

Thursday _____

Goal Tasks

Schedual Notes

_____
_____
_____
_____

Productivity Score

Routine Tasks completed ①②③④⑤⑥⑦⑧⑨⑩

Friday _____   **Goal Tasks**

Schedual Notes   _____
                            _____
                            _____
                            _____

                            Productivity Score
Routine Tasks completed ① ② ③ ④ ⑤ ⑥ ⑦ ⑧ ⑨ ⑩

Saturday _____ **Goal Tasks**

Schedual Notes   _____
                            _____
                            _____
                            _____

                            Productivity Score
Routine Tasks completed ① ② ③ ④ ⑤ ⑥ ⑦ ⑧ ⑨ ⑩

Sunday _____   **Goal Tasks**

Schedual Notes   _____
                            _____
                            _____
                            _____

                            Productivity Score
Routine Tasks completed ① ② ③ ④ ⑤ ⑥ ⑦ ⑧ ⑨ ⑩

Weekly Reflection

Weekly wins; What went well?

What routine tasks or goal tasks were not completed and why?

What have you learned? What would you change?

1 PETER 5:7
CASTING ALL YOUR ANXIETIES ON HIM,
BECAUSE HE CARES FOR YOU.

Week: _____

Goal Tasks
(order of priority)

_____

_____

_____

_____

_____

_____

_____

_____

_____

_____

_____

_____

Routine Tasks

Monday _____   **Goal Tasks**

   Schedual Notes   _____

                        _____

                        _____

                        _____

                        Productivity Score

Routine Tasks completed ① ② ③ ④ ⑤ ⑥ ⑦ ⑧ ⑨ ⑩

Tuesday _____   **Goal Tasks**

   Schedual Notes   _____

                        _____

                        _____

                        _____

                        Productivity Score

Routine Tasks completed ① ② ③ ④ ⑤ ⑥ ⑦ ⑧ ⑨ ⑩

Wednesday_____   **Goal Tasks**

   Schedual Notes   _____

                        _____

                        _____

                        _____

                        Productivity Score

Routine Tasks completed ① ② ③ ④ ⑤ ⑥ ⑦ ⑧ ⑨ ⑩

Thursday _____   **Goal Tasks**

   Schedual Notes   _____

                        _____

                        _____

                        _____

                        Productivity Score

Routine Tasks completed ① ② ③ ④ ⑤ ⑥ ⑦ ⑧ ⑨ ⑩

Friday _____   **Goal Tasks**

    Schedual Notes
_____
_____
_____
_____

Productivity Score

Routine Tasks completed ①②③④⑤⑥⑦⑧⑨⑩

Saturday _____   **Goal Tasks**

    Schedual Notes
_____
_____
_____
_____

Productivity Score

Routine Tasks completed ①②③④⑤⑥⑦⑧⑨⑩

Sunday _____   **Goal Tasks**

    Schedual Notes
_____
_____
_____
_____

Productivity Score

Routine Tasks completed ①②③④⑤⑥⑦⑧⑨⑩

Weekly Reflection

Weekly wins; What went well?

What routine tasks or goal tasks were not completed and why?

What have you learned? What would you change?

JOHN 3:16
"FOR GOD SO LOVED THE WORLD, THAT HE GAVE HIS ONLY SON, THAT WHOEVER BELIEVES IN HIM SHOULD NOT PERISH BUT HAVE ETERNAL LIFE.

Week: _____

Goal Tasks (order of priority)	Routine Tasks
_____	
_____	
_____	
_____	
_____	
_____	
_____	
_____	
_____	
_____	
_____	
_____	
_____	

Monday _____ **Goal Tasks**

Schedual Notes _____
_____
_____
_____

Productivity Score

Routine Tasks completed ① ② ③ ④ ⑤ ⑥ ⑦ ⑧ ⑨ ⑩

Tuesday _____ **Goal Tasks**

Schedual Notes _____
_____
_____
_____

Productivity Score

Routine Tasks completed ① ② ③ ④ ⑤ ⑥ ⑦ ⑧ ⑨ ⑩

Wednesday_____ **Goal Tasks**

Schedual Notes _____
_____
_____
_____

Productivity Score

Routine Tasks completed ① ② ③ ④ ⑤ ⑥ ⑦ ⑧ ⑨ ⑩

Thursday _____ **Goal Tasks**

Schedual Notes _____
_____
_____
_____

Productivity Score

Routine Tasks completed ① ② ③ ④ ⑤ ⑥ ⑦ ⑧ ⑨ ⑩

Friday _____   **Goal Tasks**

     Schedual Notes
                                                                _____

Productivity Score

Routine Tasks completed ① ② ③ ④ ⑤ ⑥ ⑦ ⑧ ⑨ ⑩

Saturday _____   **Goal Tasks**

     Schedual Notes

Productivity Score

Routine Tasks completed ① ② ③ ④ ⑤ ⑥ ⑦ ⑧ ⑨ ⑩

Sunday _____   **Goal Tasks**

     Schedual Notes

Productivity Score

Routine Tasks completed ① ② ③ ④ ⑤ ⑥ ⑦ ⑧ ⑨ ⑩

Weekly Reflection

Weekly wins; What went well?

What routine tasks or goal tasks were not completed and why?

What have you learned? What would you change?

Week: _____

Goal Tasks
(order of priority)

Routine Tasks

_____
_____
_____
_____
_____
_____
_____
_____
_____
_____
_____
_____
_____
_____

Monday _____   **Goal Tasks**

   Schedual Notes   _____
                                     _____
                                     _____
                                     _____

                              Productivity Score

Routine Tasks completed ①②③④⑤⑥⑦⑧⑨⑩

Tuesday _____   **Goal Tasks**

   Schedual Notes   _____
                                     _____
                                     _____
                                     _____

                              Productivity Score

Routine Tasks completed ①②③④⑤⑥⑦⑧⑨⑩

Wednesday_____   **Goal Tasks**

   Schedual Notes   _____
                                     _____
                                     _____
                                     _____

                              Productivity Score

Routine Tasks completed ①②③④⑤⑥⑦⑧⑨⑩

Thursday _____   **Goal Tasks**

   Schedual Notes   _____
                                     _____
                                     _____
                                     _____

                              Productivity Score

Routine Tasks completed ①②③④⑤⑥⑦⑧⑨⑩

Friday _____   **Goal Tasks**

    Schedual Notes   _____
                                _____
                                _____
                                _____

                                Productivity Score

Routine Tasks completed ① ② ③ ④ ⑤ ⑥ ⑦ ⑧ ⑨ ⑩

Saturday _____   **Goal Tasks**

    Schedual Notes   _____
                                _____
                                _____
                                _____

                                Productivity Score

Routine Tasks completed ① ② ③ ④ ⑤ ⑥ ⑦ ⑧ ⑨ ⑩

Sunday _____   **Goal Tasks**

    Schedual Notes   _____
                                _____
                                _____
                                _____

                                Productivity Score

Routine Tasks completed ① ② ③ ④ ⑤ ⑥ ⑦ ⑧ ⑨ ⑩

Weekly Reflection

Weekly wins; What went well?

What routine tasks or goal tasks were not completed and why?

What have you learned? What would you change?

Month: _____

Sunday	Monday	Tuesday	Wednesday	Thursday	Friday	Saturday

Monthly Goals

_____
_____

Goal   Tasks

_____
_____
_____
_____
_____

_____
_____

Goal   Tasks

_____
_____
_____
_____
_____

_____
_____

Goal   Tasks

_____
_____
_____
_____

Monthly Goals

Goal

Tasks

Goal

Tasks

Goal

Tasks

JOHN 14:27

PEACE I LEAVE WITH YOU; MY PEACE I GIVE TO YOU. NOT AS THE WORLD GIVES DO I GIVE TO YOU. LET NOT YOUR HEARTS BE TROUBLED, NEITHER LET THEM BE AFRAID.

Week: _____

Goal Tasks (order of priority)	Routine Tasks
_____	
_____	
_____	
_____	
_____	
_____	
_____	
_____	
_____	
_____	
_____	
_____	
_____	
_____	

Monday _____

Schedual Notes

Goal Tasks

_____

_____

_____

_____

Productivity Score

Routine Tasks completed ① ② ③ ④ ⑤ ⑥ ⑦ ⑧ ⑨ ⑩

Tuesday _____

Schedual Notes

Goal Tasks

_____

_____

_____

_____

Productivity Score

Routine Tasks completed ① ② ③ ④ ⑤ ⑥ ⑦ ⑧ ⑨ ⑩

Wednesday _____

Schedual Notes

Goal Tasks

_____

_____

_____

_____

Productivity Score

Routine Tasks completed ① ② ③ ④ ⑤ ⑥ ⑦ ⑧ ⑨ ⑩

Thursday _____

Schedual Notes

Goal Tasks

_____

_____

_____

_____

Productivity Score

Routine Tasks completed ① ② ③ ④ ⑤ ⑥ ⑦ ⑧ ⑨ ⑩

Friday _____

Goal Tasks

Schedual Notes

_____
_____
_____
_____

Productivity Score

Routine Tasks completed ①②③④⑤⑥⑦⑧⑨⑩

Saturday _____

Goal Tasks

Schedual Notes

_____
_____
_____
_____

Productivity Score

Routine Tasks completed ①②③④⑤⑥⑦⑧⑨⑩

Sunday _____

Goal Tasks

Schedual Notes

_____
_____
_____
_____

Productivity Score

Routine Tasks completed ①②③④⑤⑥⑦⑧⑨⑩

Weekly Reflection

Weekly wins; What went well?

What routine tasks or goal tasks were not completed and why?

What have you learned? What would you change?

PSALM 1:3
HE IS LIKE A TREE PLANTED BY STREAMS OF WATER THAT YIELDS ITS FRUIT IN ITS SEASON, AND ITS LEAF DOES NOT WITHER. IN ALL THAT HE DOES, HE PROSPERS.

Week: _____

Goal Tasks
(order of priority)

_____

_____

_____

_____

_____

_____

_____

_____

_____

_____

_____

Routine Tasks

Monday _____   **Goal Tasks**

    Schedual Notes
                                       _____
                                       _____
                                       _____
                                       _____

                                    Productivity Score

Routine Tasks completed ① ② ③ ④ ⑤ ⑥ ⑦ ⑧ ⑨ ⑩

Tuesday _____   **Goal Tasks**

    Schedual Notes
                                       _____
                                       _____
                                       _____
                                       _____

                                    Productivity Score

Routine Tasks completed ① ② ③ ④ ⑤ ⑥ ⑦ ⑧ ⑨ ⑩

Wednesday _____   **Goal Tasks**

    Schedual Notes
                                       _____
                                       _____
                                       _____
                                       _____

                                    Productivity Score

Routine Tasks completed ① ② ③ ④ ⑤ ⑥ ⑦ ⑧ ⑨ ⑩

Thursday _____   **Goal Tasks**

    Schedual Notes
                                       _____
                                       _____
                                       _____
                                       _____

                                    Productivity Score

Routine Tasks completed ① ② ③ ④ ⑤ ⑥ ⑦ ⑧ ⑨ ⑩

Friday _____

Goal Tasks

Schedual Notes

_____

_____

_____

_____

Productivity Score

Routine Tasks completed ①②③④⑤⑥⑦⑧⑨⑩

Saturday _____

Goal Tasks

Schedual Notes

_____

_____

_____

_____

Productivity Score

Routine Tasks completed ①②③④⑤⑥⑦⑧⑨⑩

Sunday _____

Goal Tasks

Schedual Notes

_____

_____

_____

_____

Productivity Score

Routine Tasks completed ①②③④⑤⑥⑦⑧⑨⑩

Weekly Reflection

Weekly wins; What went well?

What routine tasks or goal tasks were not completed and why?

What have you learned? What would you change?

JAMES 1:5
IF ANY OF YOU LACKS WISDOM, LET HIM ASK GOD, WHO GIVES GENEROUSLY TO ALL WITHOUT REPROACH, AND IT WILL BE GIVEN HIM.

Week: _____

Goal Tasks	Routine Tasks
(order of priority)	

Goal Tasks
(order of priority)

_____
_____
_____
_____
_____
_____
_____
_____
_____
_____
_____
_____
_____

Monday _____   **Goal Tasks**

   Schedual Notes   _____

                                                _____

                                                _____

                                                _____

                                                Productivity Score

Routine Tasks completed ①②③④⑤⑥⑦⑧⑨⑩

Tuesday _____   **Goal Tasks**

   Schedual Notes   _____

                                                _____

                                                _____

                                                _____

                                                Productivity Score

Routine Tasks completed ①②③④⑤⑥⑦⑧⑨⑩

Wednesday _____   **Goal Tasks**

   Schedual Notes   _____

                                                _____

                                                _____

                                                _____

                                                Productivity Score

Routine Tasks completed ①②③④⑤⑥⑦⑧⑨⑩

Thursday _____   **Goal Tasks**

   Schedual Notes   _____

                                                _____

                                                _____

                                                _____

                                                Productivity Score

Routine Tasks completed ①②③④⑤⑥⑦⑧⑨⑩

Friday _____   **Goal Tasks**

   Schedual Notes
                                      _____
                                      _____
                                      _____

                                      Productivity Score

Routine Tasks completed ①②③④⑤⑥⑦⑧⑨⑩

Saturday _____   **Goal Tasks**

   Schedual Notes
                                        _____
                                      _____
                                      _____

                                      Productivity Score

Routine Tasks completed ①②③④⑤⑥⑦⑧⑨⑩

Sunday _____   **Goal Tasks**

   Schedual Notes
                                        _____
                                      _____
                                      _____

                                      Productivity Score

Routine Tasks completed ①②③④⑤⑥⑦⑧⑨⑩

Weekly Reflection

Weekly wins; What went well?

What routine tasks or goal tasks were not completed and why?

What have you learned? What would you change?

DEUTERONOMY 31:6
BE STRONG AND COURAGEOUS. DO NOT FEAR OR BE IN DREAD OF THEM, FOR IT IS THE LORD YOUR GOD WHO GOES WITH YOU. HE WILL NOT LEAVE YOU OR FORSAKE YOU."

Week: _____

Goal Tasks
(order of priority)

Routine Tasks

_____

_____

_____

_____

_____

_____

_____

_____

_____

_____

_____

_____

Monday _____ **Goal Tasks**

    Schedual Notes
_____

_____

_____

_____

Productivity Score

Routine Tasks completed ①②③④⑤⑥⑦⑧⑨⑩

Tuesday _____ **Goal Tasks**

    Schedual Notes
_____

_____

_____

_____

Productivity Score

Routine Tasks completed ①②③④⑤⑥⑦⑧⑨⑩

Wednesday_____ **Goal Tasks**

    Schedual Notes
_____

_____

_____

_____

Productivity Score

Routine Tasks completed ①②③④⑤⑥⑦⑧⑨⑩

Thursday _____ **Goal Tasks**

    Schedual Notes
_____

_____

_____

_____

Productivity Score

Routine Tasks completed ①②③④⑤⑥⑦⑧⑨⑩

Friday _____

Goal Tasks

_____
_____
_____
_____

Productivity Score

Routine Tasks completed ①②③④⑤⑥⑦⑧⑨⑩

Saturday _____

Schedual Notes

Goal Tasks

_____
_____
_____
_____

Productivity Score

Routine Tasks completed ①②③④⑤⑥⑦⑧⑨⑩

Sunday _____

Schedual Notes

Goal Tasks

_____
_____
_____
_____

Productivity Score

Routine Tasks completed ①②③④⑤⑥⑦⑧⑨⑩

Weekly Reflection

Weekly wins; What went well?

What routine tasks or goal tasks were not completed and why?

What have you learned? What would you change?

Month: _____

Sunday	Monday	Tuesday	Wednesday	Thursday	Friday	Saturday

Monthly Goals

Goal

Tasks

Goal

Tasks

Goal

Tasks

Monthly Goals

Goal

Tasks

_____
_____
_____
_____
_____

Goal

Tasks

_____
_____
_____
_____
_____

Goal

Tasks

_____
_____
_____
_____
_____

JOHN 15:7-8

IF YOU ABIDE IN ME, AND MY WORDS ABIDE IN YOU, ASK WHATEVER YOU WISH, AND IT WILL BE DONE FOR YOU. BY THIS MY FATHER IS GLORIFIED, THAT YOU BEAR MUCH FRUIT AND SO PROVE TO BE MY DISCIPLES.

Week: _____

Goal Tasks (order of priority)	Routine Tasks
_____	
_____	
_____	
_____	
_____	
_____	
_____	
_____	
_____	
_____	
_____	
_____	
_____	
_____	

Monday _____ **Goal Tasks**

    Schedual Notes
_____
_____
_____
_____

Productivity Score

Routine Tasks completed ①②③④⑤⑥⑦⑧⑨⑩

Tuesday _____ **Goal Tasks**

    Schedual Notes
_____
_____
_____
_____

Productivity Score

Routine Tasks completed ①②③④⑤⑥⑦⑧⑨⑩

Wednesday _____ **Goal Tasks**

    Schedual Notes
_____
_____
_____
_____

Productivity Score

Routine Tasks completed ①②③④⑤⑥⑦⑧⑨⑩

Thursday _____ **Goal Tasks**

    Schedual Notes
_____
_____
_____
_____

Productivity Score

Routine Tasks completed ①②③④⑤⑥⑦⑧⑨⑩

Friday _____   **Goal Tasks**

Schedual Notes   _____

                                _____

                                _____

                                _____

                                Productivity Score

Routine Tasks completed ①②③④⑤⑥⑦⑧⑨⑩

Saturday _____   **Goal Tasks**

Schedual Notes   _____

                                _____

                                _____

                                _____

                                Productivity Score

Routine Tasks completed ①②③④⑤⑥⑦⑧⑨⑩

Sunday _____   **Goal Tasks**

Schedual Notes   _____

                                _____

                                _____

                                _____

                                Productivity Score

Routine Tasks completed ①②③④⑤⑥⑦⑧⑨⑩

Weekly Reflection

Weekly wins; What went well?

What routine tasks or goal tasks were not completed and why?

What have you learned? What would you change?

Week: _____

Goal Tasks
(order of priority)

_____
_____
_____
_____
_____
_____
_____
_____
_____
_____
_____
_____

Routine Tasks

Monday _____   **Goal Tasks**

    Schedual Notes
                                       _____
                                       _____
                                       _____

Productivity Score

Routine Tasks completed ①②③④⑤⑥⑦⑧⑨⑩

Tuesday _____   **Goal Tasks**

    Schedual Notes
_____
_____
_____

Productivity Score

Routine Tasks completed ①②③④⑤⑥⑦⑧⑨⑩

Wednesday _____   **Goal Tasks**

    Schedual Notes
_____
_____
_____

Productivity Score

Routine Tasks completed ①②③④⑤⑥⑦⑧⑨⑩

Thursday _____   **Goal Tasks**

    Schedual Notes
_____
_____
_____

Productivity Score

Routine Tasks completed ①②③④⑤⑥⑦⑧⑨⑩

Friday _____ **Goal Tasks**

Schedual Notes
_____
_____
_____
_____

Productivity Score

Routine Tasks completed ①②③④⑤⑥⑦⑧⑨⑩

Saturday _____ **Goal Tasks**

Schedual Notes
_____
_____
_____
_____

Productivity Score

Routine Tasks completed ①②③④⑤⑥⑦⑧⑨⑩

Sunday _____ **Goal Tasks**

Schedual Notes
_____
_____
_____
_____

Productivity Score

Routine Tasks completed ①②③④⑤⑥⑦⑧⑨⑩

Weekly Reflection

Weekly wins; What went well?

What routine tasks or goal tasks were not completed and why?

What have you learned? What would you change?

EXODUS 14:14

**THE LORD WILL FIGHT FOR YOU, AND YOU
HAVE ONLY TO BE SILENT."**

Week: _____

Goal Tasks (order of priority)	Routine Tasks
_____	
_____	
_____	
_____	
_____	
_____	
_____	
_____	
_____	
_____	
_____	
_____	
_____	

Monday _____ **Goal Tasks**

    Schedual Notes _____

                                            _____

                                            _____

Productivity Score

Routine Tasks completed ① ② ③ ④ ⑤ ⑥ ⑦ ⑧ ⑨ ⑩

Tuesday _____ **Goal Tasks**

    Schedual Notes _____

                                            _____

                                            _____

Productivity Score

Routine Tasks completed ① ② ③ ④ ⑤ ⑥ ⑦ ⑧ ⑨ ⑩

Wednesday _____ **Goal Tasks**

    Schedual Notes _____

                                            _____

                                            _____

Productivity Score

Routine Tasks completed ① ② ③ ④ ⑤ ⑥ ⑦ ⑧ ⑨ ⑩

Thursday _____ **Goal Tasks**

    Schedual Notes _____

                                            _____

                                            _____

Productivity Score

Routine Tasks completed ① ② ③ ④ ⑤ ⑥ ⑦ ⑧ ⑨ ⑩

Friday _____   **Goal Tasks**

    Schedual Notes
                                 _____
                                 _____
                                 _____
                                 _____

Productivity Score

Routine Tasks completed ①②③④⑤⑥⑦⑧⑨⑩

Saturday _____   **Goal Tasks**

    Schedual Notes
                                 _____
                                 _____
                                 _____
                                 _____

Productivity Score

Routine Tasks completed ①②③④⑤⑥⑦⑧⑨⑩

Sunday _____   **Goal Tasks**

    Schedual Notes
                                 _____
                                 _____
                                 _____
                                 _____

Productivity Score

Routine Tasks completed ①②③④⑤⑥⑦⑧⑨⑩

Weekly Reflection

Weekly wins; What went well?

What routine tasks or goal tasks were not completed and why?

What have you learned? What would you change?

HEBREWS 13:5
KEEP YOUR LIFE FREE FROM LOVE OF MONEY, AND BE CONTENT WITH WHAT YOU HAVE, FOR HE HAS SAID, "I WILL NEVER LEAVE YOU NOR FORSAKE YOU."

Week: _____

Goal Tasks (order of priority)	Routine Tasks
_____	
_____	
_____	
_____	
_____	
_____	
_____	
_____	
_____	
_____	
_____	
_____	
_____	

Monday _____

    Schedual Notes

Goal Tasks

_____

_____

_____

_____

Productivity Score

Routine Tasks completed ①②③④⑤⑥⑦⑧⑨⑩

Tuesday _____

    Schedual Notes

Goal Tasks

_____

_____

_____

_____

Productivity Score

Routine Tasks completed ①②③④⑤⑥⑦⑧⑨⑩

Wednesday_____

    Schedual Notes

Goal Tasks

_____

_____

_____

_____

Productivity Score

Routine Tasks completed ①②③④⑤⑥⑦⑧⑨⑩

Thursday _____

    Schedual Notes

Goal Tasks

_____

_____

_____

_____

Productivity Score

Routine Tasks completed ①②③④⑤⑥⑦⑧⑨⑩

Friday _____   **Goal Tasks**

Schedual Notes   _____
                                  _____
                                  _____
                                  _____

                                  Productivity Score
Routine Tasks completed ①②③④⑤⑥⑦⑧⑨⑩

Saturday _____   **Goal Tasks**

Schedual Notes   _____
                                  _____
                                  _____
                                  _____

                                  Productivity Score
Routine Tasks completed ①②③④⑤⑥⑦⑧⑨⑩

Sunday _____   **Goal Tasks**

Schedual Notes   _____
                                  _____
                                  _____
                                  _____

                                  Productivity Score
Routine Tasks completed ①②③④⑤⑥⑦⑧⑨⑩

Weekly Reflection

Weekly wins; What went well?

What routine tasks or goal tasks were not completed and why?

What have you learned? What would you change?

Month: _____

Sunday	Monday	Tuesday	Wednesday	Thursday	Friday	Saturday

Monthly Goals

Dream

_____

_____

Goal   Tasks

_____

_____

_____

_____

_____

_____

Dream

_____

_____

Goal   Tasks

_____

_____

_____

_____

_____

_____

Dream

_____

_____

Goal   Tasks

_____

_____

_____

_____

_____

Monthly Goals

Goal

Tasks

Goal

Tasks

Goal

Tasks

LUKE 11:13

IF YOU THEN, WHO ARE EVIL, KNOW HOW TO GIVE GOOD GIFTS TO
YOUR CHILDREN, HOW MUCH MORE WILL THE HEAVENLY FATHER
GIVE THE HOLY SPIRIT TO THOSE WHO ASK HIM!"

Week: _____

Goal Tasks (order of priority)	Routine Tasks
_____	
_____	
_____	
_____	
_____	
_____	
_____	
_____	
_____	
_____	
_____	
_____	
_____	
_____	

Monday _____

Schedual Notes

Goal Tasks

_____
_____
_____
_____

Productivity Score

Routine Tasks completed ①②③④⑤⑥⑦⑧⑨⑩

Tuesday _____

Schedual Notes

Goal Tasks

_____
_____
_____
_____

Productivity Score

Routine Tasks completed ①②③④⑤⑥⑦⑧⑨⑩

Wednesday _____

Schedual Notes

Goal Tasks

_____
_____
_____
_____

Productivity Score

Routine Tasks completed ①②③④⑤⑥⑦⑧⑨⑩

Thursday _____

Schedual Notes

Goal Tasks

_____
_____
_____
_____

Productivity Score

Routine Tasks completed ①②③④⑤⑥⑦⑧⑨⑩

Friday _____ **Goal Tasks**

    Schedual Notes
                                             _____
                                             _____
                                             _____
                                             _____

                                           Productivity Score

Routine Tasks completed ① ② ③ ④ ⑤ ⑥ ⑦ ⑧ ⑨ ⑩

Saturday _____ **Goal Tasks**

    Schedual Notes
                                             _____
                                             _____
                                             _____
                                             _____

                                           Productivity Score

Routine Tasks completed ① ② ③ ④ ⑤ ⑥ ⑦ ⑧ ⑨ ⑩

Sunday _____ **Goal Tasks**

    Schedual Notes
                                             _____
                                           _____
                                           _____
                                           _____

                                           Productivity Score

Routine Tasks completed ① ② ③ ④ ⑤ ⑥ ⑦ ⑧ ⑨ ⑩

Weekly Reflection

Weekly wins; What went well?

What routine tasks or goal tasks were not completed and why?

What have you learned? What would you change?

JAMES 4:7

SUBMIT YOURSELVES THEREFORE TO GOD.

RESIST THE DEVIL, AND HE WILL FLEE FROM YOU.

Week: _____

Goal Tasks
(order of priority)

_____
_____
_____
_____
_____
_____
_____
_____
_____
_____
_____
_____
_____

Routine Tasks

Monday _____

    Schedual Notes

Goal Tasks

_____

_____

_____

_____

Productivity Score

Routine Tasks completed ①②③④⑤⑥⑦⑧⑨⑩

Tuesday _____

    Schedual Notes

Goal Tasks

_____

_____

_____

_____

Productivity Score

Routine Tasks completed ①②③④⑤⑥⑦⑧⑨⑩

Wednesday _____

    Schedual Notes

Goal Tasks

_____

_____

_____

_____

Productivity Score

Routine Tasks completed ①②③④⑤⑥⑦⑧⑨⑩

Thursday _____

    Schedual Notes

Goal Tasks

_____

_____

_____

_____

Productivity Score

Routine Tasks completed ①②③④⑤⑥⑦⑧⑨⑩

Friday _____   **Goal Tasks**

Schedual Notes   _____
                             _____
                             _____
                             _____

                             Productivity Score
Routine Tasks completed ① ② ③ ④ ⑤ ⑥ ⑦ ⑧ ⑨ ⑩

Saturday _____   **Goal Tasks**

Schedual Notes   _____
                             _____
                             _____
                             _____

                             Productivity Score
Routine Tasks completed ① ② ③ ④ ⑤ ⑥ ⑦ ⑧ ⑨ ⑩

Sunday _____   **Goal Tasks**

Schedual Notes   _____
                             _____
                             _____
                             _____

                             Productivity Score
Routine Tasks completed ① ② ③ ④ ⑤ ⑥ ⑦ ⑧ ⑨ ⑩

Weekly Reflection

Weekly wins; What went well?

What routine tasks or goal tasks were not completed and why?

What have you learned? What would you change?

Week: _____

Goal Tasks
(order of priority)

_____
_____
_____
_____
_____
_____
_____
_____
_____
_____
_____
_____
_____

Routine Tasks

Monday _____

    Schedual Notes

Goal Tasks

_____

_____

_____

Productivity Score

Routine Tasks completed ① ② ③ ④ ⑤ ⑥ ⑦ ⑧ ⑨ ⑩

Tuesday _____

    Schedual Notes

Goal Tasks

_____

_____

_____

Productivity Score

Routine Tasks completed ① ② ③ ④ ⑤ ⑥ ⑦ ⑧ ⑨ ⑩

Wednesday _____

    Schedual Notes

Goal Tasks

_____

_____

_____

Productivity Score

Routine Tasks completed ① ② ③ ④ ⑤ ⑥ ⑦ ⑧ ⑨ ⑩

Thursday _____

    Schedual Notes

Goal Tasks

_____

_____

_____

Productivity Score

Routine Tasks completed ① ② ③ ④ ⑤ ⑥ ⑦ ⑧ ⑨ ⑩

Friday _____   **Goal Tasks**

    Schedual Notes   _____
                                  _____
                                  _____
                                  _____

                                  Productivity Score

Routine Tasks completed ① ② ③ ④ ⑤ ⑥ ⑦ ⑧ ⑨ ⑩

Saturday _____   **Goal Tasks**

    Schedual Notes   _____
                                  _____
                                  _____
                                  _____

                                  Productivity Score

Routine Tasks completed ① ② ③ ④ ⑤ ⑥ ⑦ ⑧ ⑨ ⑩

Sunday _____   **Goal Tasks**

    Schedual Notes   _____
                                  _____
                                  _____
                                  _____

                                  Productivity Score

Routine Tasks completed ① ② ③ ④ ⑤ ⑥ ⑦ ⑧ ⑨ ⑩

Weekly Reflection

Weekly wins; What went well?

What routine tasks or goal tasks were not completed and why?

What have you learned? What would you change?

LUKE 18:27

BUT HE SAID, "WHAT IS IMPOSSIBLE
WITH MEN IS POSSIBLE WITH GOD."

Week: _____

Goal Tasks
(order of priority)

_____
_____
_____
_____
_____
_____
_____
_____
_____
_____
_____
_____
_____
_____

Routine Tasks

Monday _____

Goal Tasks

Schedual Notes

_____
_____
_____
_____

Productivity Score

Routine Tasks completed ①②③④⑤⑥⑦⑧⑨⑩

Tuesday _____

Goal Tasks

Schedual Notes

_____
_____
_____
_____

Productivity Score

Routine Tasks completed ①②③④⑤⑥⑦⑧⑨⑩

Wednesday_____

Goal Tasks

Schedual Notes

_____
_____
_____
_____

Productivity Score

Routine Tasks completed ①②③④⑤⑥⑦⑧⑨⑩

Thursday _____

Goal Tasks

Schedual Notes

_____
_____
_____
_____

Productivity Score

Routine Tasks completed ①②③④⑤⑥⑦⑧⑨⑩

Friday _____

Goal Tasks

Schedual Notes

_____
_____
_____
_____

Productivity Score

Routine Tasks completed ① ② ③ ④ ⑤ ⑥ ⑦ ⑧ ⑨ ⑩

Saturday _____

Goal Tasks

Schedual Notes

_____
_____
_____
_____

Productivity Score

Routine Tasks completed ① ② ③ ④ ⑤ ⑥ ⑦ ⑧ ⑨ ⑩

Sunday _____

Goal Tasks

Schedual Notes

_____
_____
_____
_____

Productivity Score

Routine Tasks completed ① ② ③ ④ ⑤ ⑥ ⑦ ⑧ ⑨ ⑩

Weekly Reflection

Weekly wins; What went well?

What routine tasks or goal tasks were not completed and why?

What have you learned? What would you change?

Notes

Notes

Notes